Beginning Backup and Restore for SQL Server

Data Loss Management and Prevention Techniques

Bradley Beard

Apress®

Beginning Backup and Restore for SQL Server

Bradley Beard
Palm Bay, Florida, USA

ISBN-13 (pbk): 978-1-4842-3455-6   ISBN-13 (electronic): 978-1-4842-3456-3
https://doi.org/10.1007/978-1-4842-3456-3

Library of Congress Control Number: 2018947418

Managing Director, Apress Media LLC: Welmoed Spahr
Acquisitions Editor: Jonathan Gennick
Development Editor: Laura Berendson
Coordinating Editor: Jill Balzano

Cover designed by eStudioCalamar

Cover image designed by Freepik (www.freepik.com)

Distributed to the book trade worldwide by Springer Science+Business Media New York, 233 Spring Street, 6th Floor, New York, NY 10013. Phone 1-800-SPRINGER, fax (201) 348-4505, e-mail orders-ny@springer-sbm.com, or visit www.springeronline.com. Apress Media, LLC is a California LLC and the sole member (owner) is Springer Science + Business Media Finance Inc (SSBM Finance Inc). SSBM Finance Inc is a **Delaware** corporation.

For information on translations, please e-mail rights@apress.com, or visit http://www.apress.com/rights-permissions.

Apress titles may be purchased in bulk for academic, corporate, or promotional use. eBook versions and licenses are also available for most titles. For more information, reference our Print and eBook Bulk Sales web page at http://www.apress.com/bulk-sales.

Any source code or other supplementary material referenced by the author in this book is available to readers on GitHub via the book's product page, located at www.apress.com/9781484234556. For more detailed information, please visit http://www.apress.com/source-code.

Printed on acid-free paper

*For Kim and Zaria, Melissa and Blake,
all my family and friends, and
most importantly... you.*

Table of Contents

About the Author

 **Bradley Beard** is a professional software developer in Palm Bay, Florida. He started off designing websites using PHP and MySQL in the late 90s, and gradually moved to ColdFusion and SQL Server. He earned his MCSA: SQL Server 2012 certification in July 2013, and his MCSE: Business Intelligence certification in February 2016. He was the Technical Reviewer for Mike McQuillan's book, *Introducing SQL Server,* as well as the author of his own book, *Practical Maintenance Plans in SQL Server,* both available from Apress. He then went on to write his second book, *Beginning SQL Server R Services,* also available from Apress.

About the Technical Reviewer

 **Rodney Landrum** went to school to be a poet and a writer. And then he graduated, so that dream was crushed. He followed another path, which was to become a professional in the fun-filled world of information technology. He has worked as a systems engineer, UNIX and network admin, data analyst, client services director, and finally database administrator. The old hankering to put words on paper, while paper still existed, got the best of him, and in 2000, he began writing technical articles—some creative and humorous, some quite the opposite. In 2010 he wrote *The SQL Server Tacklebox*, a title his editor disdained but a book closest to the true creative potential he sought; he wanted to do a full book without a single screenshot. He promises his next book will be fiction or a collection of poetry, but that has yet to transpire.

Acknowledgments

Thanks to Jonathan and Jill at Apress for letting me write another book.

Thanks to my "newly retired" parents for everything.

Finally, thanks to my wife and kids for understanding.

Introduction to Backup and Restore Methodologies

As database administrators, our primary duty is to protect the data in the databases we are responsible for. This data represents the heart and soul of the company employing us, and could destroy a business if not maintained properly. In this context, the proper application of a sound backup and restore solution is absolutely necessary to provide another level of data security in the event of a catastrophe. We need to be able to ensure that data can be restored in the case of an emergency, and the only way to ensure a smooth restoration of data is to ensure that there has been a correct backup of the data needing to be restored.

There is no way to restore data that has not been backed up in some fashion. Luckily, there are quite a few ways that data can be backed up, both inside of and outside of SQL Server. For this book, we will be dealing strictly with the SQL Server administrator aspect of backing up and restoring data, and not viewing this topic from the Windows Server administrator point of view. Additionally, we will not be getting very deeply into advanced practices beyond SQL Server Management Studio. The reason for this is because I want to keep as much attention on the actual tool used for development and maintenance as possible. In order to do that, I need to make as much of the book as possible directly related to SSMS. Please note that this does not mean that you are forever married to the concept of only using SQL Server Management Studio to manage your database backups; that is not the case. Rather, I want to introduce concepts in this book that will hopefully expand your understanding of what backups and restores are and how they can be properly maintained in the context of SQL Server. This does mean, however, that we are going to stay well within the confines of SQL Server. To be absolutely clear, we are not going to get into different storage techniques separate from how SQL Server prepares and delivers a backup solution to a predefined storage location, and then how SQL Server retrieves that backup solution in order to restore damaged, missing, or corrupted data. Instead, we are going to focus on the myriad of different settings and techniques that can be employed to make sure that the backup set you get is what is expected. Consequently, we will also be looking at various different restoration techniques available within SQL Server as well.

Note   When a backup is created by SQL Server, you can choose from a variety of options to detail exactly what data to include in a backup. When a backup is created by Windows, the entire database file is backed up along with the file system. This can be advantageous, but it is also a waste of space and sometimes impossible to restore, if encrypted.

Specifically, this book will address the following items, among many other topics:

- Advantages/disadvantages and proper usage of the three main backup types

  - Full: a backup of the entire database

  - Differential: a backup of the changed information since the last full backup

  - Transaction log: the log of transactions since the last backup

- Different backup methodologies used for different-sized organizations

  - Onsite vs. offsite storage

  - Data retention periods

  - Storage mediums and inherent differences (tapes vs. USB vs. DVD)

- Compression types for backups

- Encryption types for backups

It is important to note that we will be preparing many backup solutions in the course of this book, and the solutions we create will be on a single physical hard drive partitioned into multiple logical hard drives. If you have read any of my other books, you will know that I have a specific way of setting up my SQL Server file locations, as shown in Listing 1. To me, this helps to organize the folder structure logically, as opposed to diving into the quagmire of nested folders to reach the default file and folder locations.

Listing 1. File Locations

```
Folder Location          Purpose
E:\SQL Server\Backups    Backup (.bak) files
E:\SQL Server\Data           Data (.mdf) files
E:\SQL Server\Logs           Log (.ldf and .trn) files
E:\SQL Server\Temp           Any other file type
```

You are free to have your system set up however you would like, of course.

For the purposes of this book, we are going to concentrate on various backup types, different restore procedures (point in time using transaction logs vs. loading a complete backup), and what components make up each procedure. We are not going to get into saving the backup files to any location other than the backups folder specified in Listing 1. Your specific scenario can be adjusted to fit your need, but the instructions in these chapters will provide you with a step-by-step instruction guide to a workable backup and restore solution. In short, this book will hopefully address nearly every issue related to backing up or restoring data, and if it doesn't completely answer the question, then it will possibly be able to point you in the right direction for your own solution.

We are going to start with a completely fresh installation of SQL Server 2016 and SQL Server Management Studio. I am not going to include SQL Server or SSMS installation instructions, since it is assumed that you already have a database up and running and that you would like to either start a backup/restore solution for it, or enhance your current backup/restore scenario.

As always, I **strongly** recommend setting up a development environment that you can use to test with. SQL Server Express is free for developers, so that's a great option. Microsoft also has some fantastic deals on Azure storage, if you don't have a local database to play with, and they are really well priced for what you get. The newest release of SQL Server Management Studio will only connect to the most "modern" version of the SQL Server engine, so keep in mind that you can connect to any previous version of SQL Server shown:

- SQL Server 2008
- SQL Server 2008 R2
- SQL Server 2012
- SQL Server 2014
- SQL Server 2016
- SQL Server 2017
- Microsoft Azure

Just about any Open Database Connectivity (ODBC) data source can be accessed through SSMS, but I would stick with Microsoft if I were you. For the sake of the exercises and the large part of the content in this book, if you decide to use something other than SQL Server or Azure, it's going to be difficult for you to follow along with exactly what is being shown.

Backup Fundamentals

Before we get started with learning about the types of backup and restore methodologies available within SQL Server, we need to understand the various parts of a backup and restore, separately and conjoined, in order to really know what we want to achieve from a backup/restore solution. It is entirely possible that your database could run smoothly for its entire life, and you will never need to restore a backup. I believe this would be the utopia for most database administrators, and I can't think of a single person that has ever had this happen for them. Most times, Murphy's Law steps in and makes sure that you either have a readily available backup to restore from, or you learn a very hard lesson in why you should have a reliable backup solution. Most of us, unfortunately, fall into this group; those database administrators that have maybe forgone the luxury of a backup solution due to time constraints or laziness, and have suffered the consequences later. If this is you, please understand that you are in good company. It is very easy to make rookie mistakes early on in your career as a database administrator, but it is expected that you learn from those mistakes so they don't happen again. That's where I would like to think that this book comes in.

When dealing with recovery of data, it is very easy to say that backups should always be available, but it is another thing altogether to know how to actually build the backup solution that you need, and have that solution available when needed. For this reason, Microsoft offers different ways of backing up data within the context of SQL Server. Let's take a look at the various pieces of backup and restore methodologies, and how they relate to each other.

Recovery Models

In SQL Server, there are three different recovery models available:

- Full

- Bulk-logged

- Simple

The purpose of these models is to give you, the database administrator, different options for how you want the backup data to be delivered. You cannot choose more than one option for one database, and you are confined to what backup type is available for each recovery model. For this reason, a recovery model should be chosen very carefully.

Think of a recovery model as the container in which the backup type, and the subsequent backup, reside. If the recovery model does not fit your needs, then you will never get the backup and restore solution you need.

Picking a recovery model is actually very simple; just decide how much data loss is acceptable for your situation, and the scenario basically builds itself. If you want very little data loss, then the simple recovery model option is discarded. This leaves the full and bulk-logged recovery models. What is the difference between these two models? Basically, the full recovery model allows for point-in-time restores, which the bulk-logged recovery model allows for backups of data only from the last restore point. Decide between those two options, and that is your desired recovery model.

The three different recovery models are discussed at length in Chapter 1.

Backup Types

Separate from recovery models are the three different backup types. Those types are as follows:

- Full: a backup of the entire database

- Differential: a backup of the changed information since the last full backup

- Transaction log: the log of transactions since the last backup

These backup types were introduced earlier in this chapter as well, and are discussed at length throughout the entirety of this book. For that reason, I won't get into the specifics of the backup types just yet, and will let the individual chapters for these areas detail the relevant information about the different types.

Note   The main idea of recovery models and backup types is that certain recovery models can only work with certain backup types, so the choice of the recovery model is the first step in designing an effective backup solution.

Keeping in mind the relationship between recovery models and backup types is important, as you can tell. The focus of this book is to reinforce that knowledge, and build on it to create a greater understanding of what we can do to create an effective backup strategy that will help mitigate disaster in the future.

PART I

Backups

CHAPTER 1

Full Backups

The concept of backing up data is one of those things that should be extremely intuitive, but is often implemented poorly, if at all. I know quite a few database administrators (DBAs) that don't worry about regular, structured backups because their database server is on a SAN (storage area network) and the data is therefore backed up regularly. To me, this makes no sense at all, since there is absolutely no contingency for point-in-time restoration of data, outside of what happened to have been backed up as part of a complete Windows backup solution. If there were a catastrophic failure, and the DBA had to rebuild the database to the point of failure, it could not be easily done. The reason is because the entire Windows image would have to be rebuilt from the last Windows backup, which means that the database will only be current to *that* particular point of time, and not the *desired* point of time. For example, if the Windows image is run nightly, but the database backups are run hourly, then you will have a perfect set of hourly backups up to the point where the Windows backup is run. If Windows fails at 11:59 PM, then that entire days' worth of database backups has been lost. The rule of thumb, generally, is to put backup files on a separate drive than the OS. This alleviates the issue outlined in the preceding, as long as the backup drive is not corrupted.

In the realm of database administration, I think it is best to imagine that your database server is a stand-alone system. This means to imagine that there is no SAN, no Windows backup solution, nothing like that at all. You must be able to manage the entire universe of your data as it pertains

© Bradley Beard 2018
B. Beard, *Beginning Backup and Restore for SQL Server*,
https://doi.org/10.1007/978-1-4842-3456-3_1

to your server. What does this entail, exactly? That's what this book will address; how to back up and restore your most important asset—the data you are responsible for.

Note   We will also briefly cover data storage techniques in this book, although that will not be a main focus. This is because, although we will highlight specific techniques for storage, it is ultimately your decision whether or not to implement storage techniques outside of what is available from your local file system.

What Is a Full Backup?

A full backup is the entirety of the data within a database from the point in time that the backup was run. Part of the transaction log is also backed up in a full backup; this is done so a successful restore can eventually be run using the backed-up data. A backup can be saved to local disk, an available network share, or even in Windows Azure blob storage (if you're running SQL Server 2012 or later). The full backup type provides the starting point for a full restore, and also the starting point for a differential restore (covered in Chapter 6) and a transaction log restore (covered in Chapter 7). In other words, without a full backup, neither a differential nor a transaction log backup can be successfully restored.

In my first book, *Practical Maintenance Plans in SQL Server* (available from Apress), I briefly discussed the concept of backups in Chapter 1, titled "Backing Up a Database." In that chapter, I went over recovery models and backup types, and then explained how to set up the maintenance task to perform these jobs automatically. For the purpose of this book, I don't think we need to go over the job creation part, but we will go over recovery models and backup types.

Recovery Models

A recovery model is how SQL Server is told to recover data. Figure 1-1 shows where to look to find the recovery model configuration area. This is found by right-clicking an existing database and choosing Properties, then selecting Options from the left menu. In the example shown, I have chosen to create a new database, so the screen you see in the figure is the New Database screen.

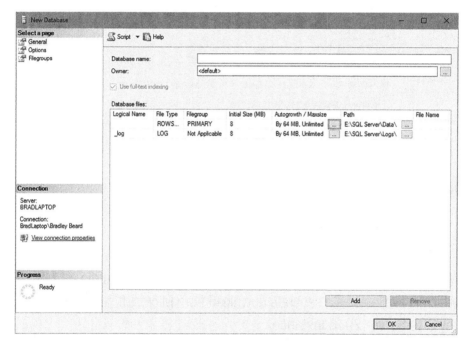

Figure 1-1. *Recovery models location in New Database screen*

I am going to name this database backrecTestDB, and this is the database that we will be using throughout this book. Obviously, you will have your own databases that you will maintain separately, but this is what we will use as a reference.

Notice that we are on the General tab, as shown in the left pane of the preceding figure. Click Options, and you should see what is shown in Figure 1-2.

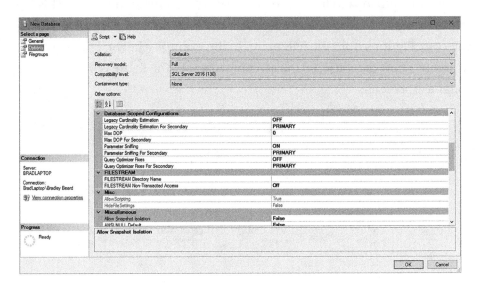

Figure 1-2. *Options*

The initial interface for the Options area is now visible.

Note   Recall that I am using SQL Server Management Studio (SSMS), which is available as a separate download from Microsoft, to administer my SQL Server 2016 instance.

At the very top of this screen, the second option down is for recovery model. You have three options for recovery models. Those options are as follows:

- Full: This option lets the database recover to nearly any point in time, and is the clear choice of many DBAs.

- Bulk-logged: Similar to full recovery, but this scenario allows for logging to be minimized for bulk operations (copying, specifically).

- Simple: This is the choice for smaller, non–mission-critical databases. It does not allow for point-in-time restores like full, or bulk operations like bulk-logged. It simply allows for recovery using the last backup.

We are going to keep the full option selected here, because we want to be able to look at point-in-time restores later on in this book.

Backup Types

SQL Server has three unique backup types, which are discussed in later chapters. They each perform differently, and they can either work together or separately to provide a backup solution for your data. The backup types that are available to you are also entirely dependent upon the recovery model used for your database. We will get more into this shortly. For now, let's take a look at Listing 1-1, which outlines the different backup types.

Listing 1-1. Backup Types

- Full backups

    - A full backup will back up the entire database, which includes the transaction log. Using this method, anything can be restored up to the point in time when the backup was run.

- Differential backups

    - A differential backup contains any data not backed up since the last full backup.

- Transaction log backups

  - A transaction log backup will contain the individual transactions that affect the current state of the database since the last backup.

There are a few things to note about these different yet similar backup types.

First, a full backup is different from a transaction log backup, in that the full backup type has the entirety of the actual data within the database, while the transaction log backup only has the individual transactions through time that affected the data contained within the database.

Second, a differential backup is useless without the last full backup. The differential backup is applied to the full backup, which creates the point-in-time restore for that particular differential backup set. One important thing to remember about differential backups is that they do not contain the transaction log, so any data beyond the differential backup will not be restored without restoring the transaction log backups.

Finally, it is important to remember that when backing up the transaction log, this releases a large chunk of memory back to the operating system, and keeps your log running smoothly. If the transaction log were never backed up, it is possible that you could have one log file that is the entire size of the hard drive the log is located on. For this reason, we can easily see that backing up the transaction log is obviously important.

How Do Recovery Models Affect the Backup Types?

Recovery models and backup types are very closely related, meaning that the choice of recovery model will determine your available options for backup types. Consider the information shown in Table 1-1.

Table 1-1. *Recovery Models and Backup Types*

	Full Recovery Model	Bulk-Logged Recovery Model	Simple Recovery Model
Backup Types	Full Differential Transaction log	Full Differential Transaction log	Full
Data Restore	Specific point in time	End of any backup	End of any backup
Data Loss	Next to none	Next to none	Since last backup

The essence here is that the full and bulk-logged recovery models can use any backup type, while the simple recovery model can only use a full backup type. The reason for this is because the simple recovery model does not support transaction log backups, which are necessary for differential backups. This obviously negates the other two backup types, leaving only the full backup type for the simple recovery model.

In terms of data restoration, the full recovery model gives the greatest level of granularity, while bulk-logged and simple both offer restoration to the end of any full or differential backup.

Finally, when dealing with data loss, we can see that full and bulk-logged recovery models offer the lowest possible loss, while simple will include data loss since the last backup.

Preparing for a Full Backup

Going back to what we saw in Figure 1-2 earlier, we can see that we have kept the recovery model at full. The rest of the settings on this page are fine to keep how they are for now, unless your particular circumstance dictates otherwise.

Since this is a new database, we don't have any tables that we can back up yet. Not to worry! Let's create some dummy data that we can use for demonstration purposes in showing how to back up data. It is safe to say that this is going to be different from your environment, because these tables and data we are going to create are not going to be business essential.

What we want to do is in four steps:

- Create tables for small bits of data

- Insert dummy data into those tables

- Use the SELECT * INTO statement to insert the data from the tables into a different table using CROSS JOIN

- Delete the original tables that held the small bits of data and just keep the master table

To create the tables, use the following script:

```
CREATE TABLE [fname] (fname [varchar](10));
CREATE TABLE [lname] (lname [varchar](10));
CREATE TABLE [animal] (animal [varchar](10));
CREATE TABLE [language] ([language] [varchar](10));
CREATE TABLE [users1] ([fname] [varchar](10), [lname] [varchar]
(10), [animal] [varchar](10), [language] [varchar](10));
CREATE TABLE [users2] ([fname] [varchar](10), [lname] [varchar]
(10), [animal] [varchar](10), [language] [varchar](10));
```

Note that we are creating two users tables here. I will get into why I am doing it like this very shortly.

Next, we want to populate those tables with dummy data. This is fairly easy, so if you have a preferred method of doing this, or are working from a backup of regular data, that is perfectly fine. We need to have ten rows of data in each table in order for this generate a decent set of data, so you can use the following code, or you can use your own.

```
INSERT INTO [fname] VALUES ('Bradley');
INSERT INTO [fname] VALUES ('Jessica');
INSERT INTO [fname] VALUES ('Josh');
INSERT INTO [fname] VALUES ('Kaylee');
INSERT INTO [fname] VALUES ('Matthew');
INSERT INTO [fname] VALUES ('Emma');
INSERT INTO [fname] VALUES ('Sommer');
INSERT INTO [fname] VALUES ('Tommy');
INSERT INTO [fname] VALUES ('Emily');
INSERT INTO [fname] VALUES ('Courtney');

INSERT INTO [lname] VALUES ('Beard');
INSERT INTO [lname] VALUES ('Jackson');
INSERT INTO [lname] VALUES ('Joseph');
INSERT INTO [lname] VALUES ('Dun');
INSERT INTO [lname] VALUES ('Hexum');
INSERT INTO [lname] VALUES ('Martinez');
INSERT INTO [lname] VALUES ('Mercury');
INSERT INTO [lname] VALUES ('May');
INSERT INTO [lname] VALUES ('Taylor');
INSERT INTO [lname] VALUES ('Deacon');

INSERT INTO [animal] VALUES ('Cat');
INSERT INTO [animal] VALUES ('Dog');
INSERT INTO [animal] VALUES ('Fish');
INSERT INTO [animal] VALUES ('Horse');
INSERT INTO [animal] VALUES ('Pig');
INSERT INTO [animal] VALUES ('Turtle');
INSERT INTO [animal] VALUES ('Guinea Pig');
INSERT INTO [animal] VALUES ('Hamster');
INSERT INTO [animal] VALUES ('Rat');
INSERT INTO [animal] VALUES ('Mouse');
```

```
INSERT INTO [language] VALUES ('English');
INSERT INTO [language] VALUES ('Spanish');
INSERT INTO [language] VALUES ('French');
INSERT INTO [language] VALUES ('Portuguese');
INSERT INTO [language] VALUES ('German');
INSERT INTO [language] VALUES ('Russian');
INSERT INTO [language] VALUES ('Slovakian');
INSERT INTO [language] VALUES ('Afrikaans');
INSERT INTO [language] VALUES ('Hindi');
INSERT INTO [language] VALUES ('Urdu');
```

That gives us four tables populated with ten rows of data in each table. Simple math tells us that, with a CROSS JOIN, we will end up with 10,000 records fairly quickly. Yes, we are breaking one of the cardinal rules of database administration and intentionally creating a Cartesian product, but it is for the purposes of creating this test data. Surely the DBA overseers will let it slide just this once.

Now that we have our data, we need to combine it into our users tables we created earlier. To do this, simply run these statements:

```
INSERT INTO users1 SELECT * FROM [fname] CROSS JOIN [lname]
CROSS JOIN [animal] CROSS JOIN [language];
INSERT INTO users2 SELECT * FROM [fname] CROSS JOIN [lname]
CROSS JOIN [animal] CROSS JOIN [language];
```

That will insert 10,000 records into each table.

To clean up (delete) the original tables, run the following code:

```
DROP TABLE [fname];
DROP TABLE [lname];
DROP TABLE [animal];
DROP TABLE [language];
```

That leaves us with just the users table left now. The next bit of code is going to run a WHILE loop 100 times and insert the values of users2 into users1 during each pass of the loop. The code looks like this:

```
DECLARE @cnt INT;
SET @cnt = 0;

WHILE @cnt <= 1000
BEGIN
        INSERT INTO users1 SELECT * FROM users2;
        SET @cnt = @cnt + 1;
END;
```

Basically, we are declaring a variable @cnt, then immediately setting it to 0. Then we set up our WHILE loop and say that as long as @cnt is less than or equal to 1000, we want to insert the values of users2 into users1 and then increment our counter. This is going to give us a ton of fake data, as you will see shortly.

Once that is complete, and it takes a few seconds to run, we need to verify that we actually have data in there that we can use, so you can easily get the count of the table by running the following script:

```
SELECT count(*) as cnt FROM users1;
```

That should show you that there are 10,020,000 records in the table now.

Note   The entire procedure for creating test data is available as a download with this book, and is titled *CreateTestData.sql*.

Now that we have a nice, big table to deal with, let's look at how we want to set up the full backup of the data.

Right-click the database name, hover over Tasks, and select Back Up, as shown in Figure 1-3.

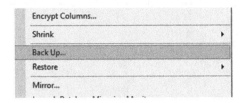

Figure 1-3. *Location of Back Up option*

Another screen opens which will allow you to manually back up a database. This screen is fairly important, so let's go over the features on each of the screens in this area.

Back Up Database: General Tab

Initially, the General tab is shown when selecting the Back Up option, as shown in Figure 1-3. This tab has selections that can be made at the highest level, with each subsequent tab from the leftmost menu drilling further into the options with more detail. Figure 1-4 shows the default settings of the General tab in my database.

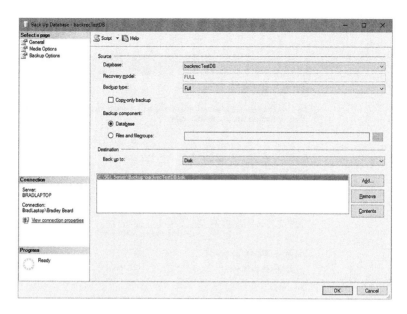

Figure 1-4. *General tab*

First, let's take a look at how our transaction log is running. A full transaction log is one of those things that will bring a database screeching to a halt, and the cause may be hard to determine unless you know what to look for. Periodic backups will keep your database running smoothly, from the point of view of the transaction log, and will also allow you to provide a heightened level of data integrity and security, which is never a bad thing.

Transaction Log Examination

Right-click the database again and select Tasks, then hover over Shrink, and finally, select the Files option. This is shown in Figure 1-5.

Figure 1-5. *Shrink Files option*

Initially, you should see what is shown in Figure 1-6.

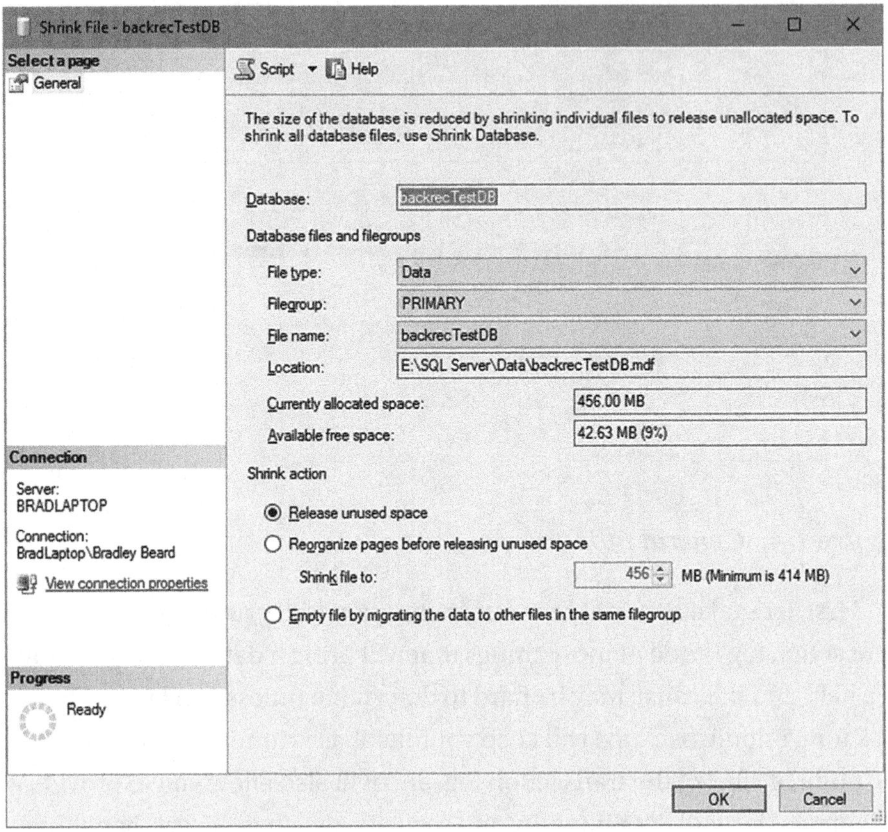

Figure 1-6. *Shrink File (Data)*

This page shows us that we can select the file type, the filegroup, and the file name for our backup. What is important is that this isn't the transaction log though; this is for the .mdf file, which is the master data file.

Pull down the File type menu and select Log from the options. The interface changes slightly and you are then shown what is in Figure 1-7.

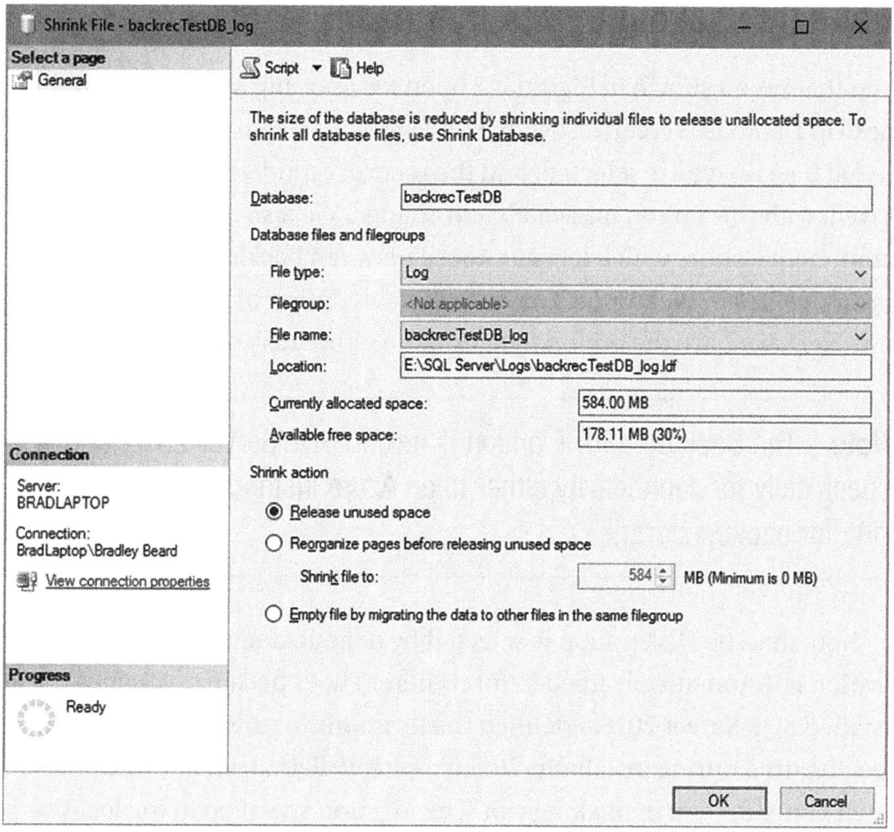

Figure 1-7. *Shrink File (Log)*

Now, we can see that this is the transaction log. This interface tells us that we have 584MB currently allocated for the transaction log, with 178.11MB available. That means that around 406MB is being used by the transaction log right now. That's not enormous, but it does leave only 30% of the currently allocated space for the transaction log to grow.

At this point, we can do one of two things: we could run a full backup, which will shrink the transaction log, or we could run a transaction log backup, which will also obviously back up the transaction log. For the purpose of this demonstration, I am going to run a full backup on the database and show what happens to the size of this transaction log.

17

Manually Backing Up the Database

Keep the screen shown in Figure 1-7 open for now, but switch back to the Back Up Database screen last shown in Figure 1-4. Here, we can see that the full backup type is selected, and the recovery model is set to FULL as well, with this option unavailable to change. We also have the backup component option, which lets us choose between backing up the database or just the files or filegroups. Leave the default option of Database selected here. Next, we have the option to back up to either disk or URL.

Note   The Back Up to URL option is new in SQL Server 2016, and is specifically for connectivity either to an Azure instance or to a remote URL for backup storage.

Note that the Disk option is selected by default, and the default location is automatically filled in for us here. That's because, when I installed SQL Server 2016, I defined the locations for the logs and backups. Take the time during installation to take care of all that, and it works out much better for you in the long run. The location specified in the location window is a valid location, and there is not a backup with that name in the file location, so this is going to be a brand-new backup; we aren't appending to an existing backup, in other words. You could click the Add button and choose another name, or click the Remove button to clear out the current option, but we'll keep it just like it is now and click OK. The options on the other tabs here aren't particularly relevant at this point, but they could be used later on for specific purposes as needed for your installation.

Once you click OK, a progress bar gives a percent status until we finally see what is shown in Figure 1-8.

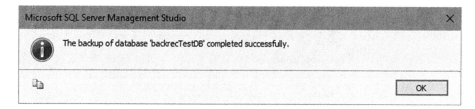

Figure 1-8. *Backup successful*

Now, let's go back to the Shrink File screen we had up a bit ago, as shown in Figure 1-7. Click the File type menu again, choose Data, and then choose Log from the same menu again. This basically refreshes the data; I suppose you could accomplish this same result by closing and reopening this window. Once the interface refreshes, we can see what is shown in Figure 1-9.

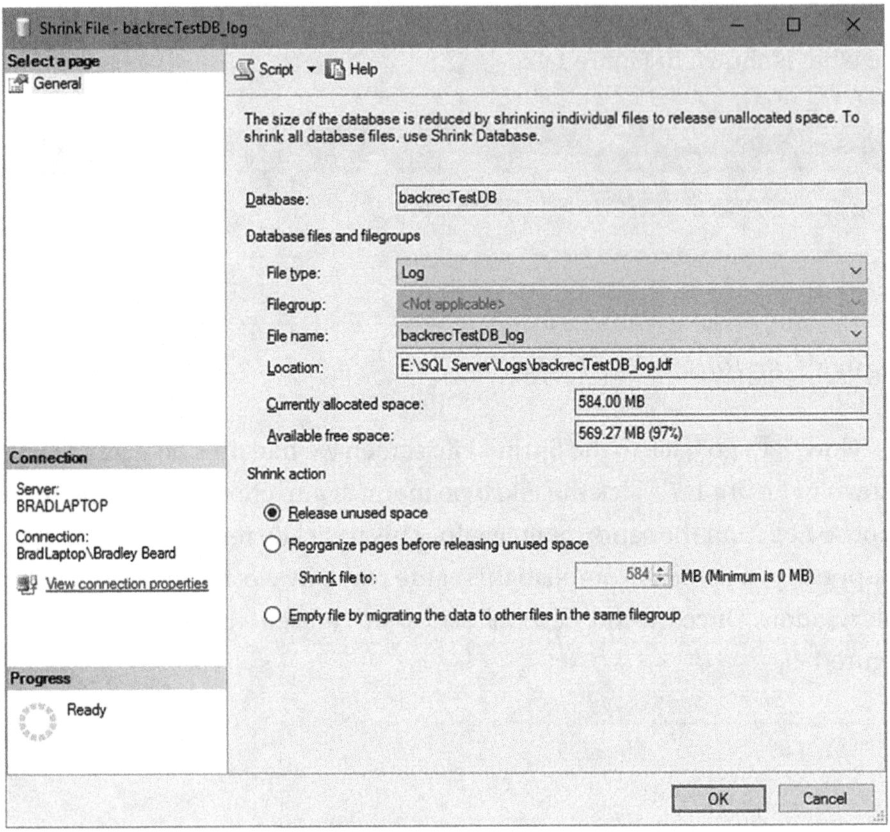

Figure 1-9. *Transaction log shrunk*

The value for available free space has gone up to 569.27MB, or 97% available. That means that this single backup operation freed up 67% of our available space for the transaction log.

Summary

This chapter walked us through an introduction to full backups, and then gave a brief demonstration of how to manually run a full backup of a database.

We can clearly see the advantage that the full backup gives us; not only does it give us an expected backup solution, but it also gives us a (mostly) fresh transaction log to work with as well. We saw how a full backup affects not only the backup being created, but also how it helps maintain the size of the transaction log so the transaction log doesn't grow out of control.

If you don't currently have a backup solution in place in your environment, these first four chapters will hopefully play an integral and essential role in your successful implementation of an extremely powerful and reliable backup system.

CHAPTER 2

Differential Backups

Setting up a structured, recurring backup does not stop with just a scheduled full backup. That is only half the battle; to be honest, a third of the battle. A good backup strategy reduces the overall risk to the data stored in the database. One of the most effective ways to reduce risk is by decreasing the total number of "links" in your backup chain (i.e., the total number of files you have to restore in the case of a disaster). Every file that gets created during a backup has a chance of being corrupted. If you have a large number of backups in a restoration, you run a greater risk of having corrupted data somewhere for that restoration cycle; the longer the chain, the greater the risk. This is where differential backups enter the backup strategy.

What Is a Differential Backup?

A differential backup captures all data residing in the database that has changed since the last full backup (also known as the *differential base*) was taken. Like the full backup, the differential backup contains transaction log data, and can back up the database as whole or specific files and filegroups. Unlike the full backup, for a differential backup to successfully execute, dependencies on other backup types have to be met.

Over the years, I have had a number of coworkers refer to differential backups synonymously as *incremental backups*; this is a common misconception, and one that can cause a DBA some trouble. In general,

© Bradley Beard 2018
B. Beard, *Beginning Backup and Restore for SQL Server*,
https://doi.org/10.1007/978-1-4842-3456-3_2

incremental backups are backups of changed data since the last backup of any type (full or differential). Differential backups are backups of changed data since the last base. What is the difference? The word "base," in this context, makes all the difference. An incremental backup will back up any data that changed since the last backup, whether it is a full or an incremental backup. The differential backup will continue to grab any data that has changed since the last full backup, regardless of how many differential backups have run. With this in mind, let's look at differential backup dependency.

Differential Backup Dependency

A differential backup has one primary dependency—a full backup. If a full backup is not successfully executed before a differential backup, then the differential backup will fail to execute.

Note   The full backup dependency will not be met by the execution of a COPY_ONLY backup. Only a traditional full backup prior to a differential backup will work. This is not to say you cannot take a COPY_ONLY backup once the traditional back is complete, only that the traditional is required.

Why Use Differential Backups?

The first question I will usually get asked when I implement a backup strategy that uses differential backups is, "What is the point of a differential when you have transactional backups? Isn't it just using more disk space?" This question often comes from someone on the infrastructure team; typically, a SAN administrator. I am not saying this to give them a hard time, as it is their job to ask these questions; I mention this to demonstrate that you will get questioned at some point on your backup strategy and why you went down the path you did.

Again, though, the question is why use differentials and not rely completely on transaction log backups. The answer can be summed up in a single word... **risk**.

It is my belief that the single most important responsibility a DBA has is protecting the data. Sure, performance, security, and maintenance are all very important and should not be overlooked. Nevertheless, the integrity and recoverability of data are paramount to any modern organization's success. This is where differentials offer their greatest value, risk mitigation for data recovery. I have stressed this point throughout each of my books, simply because there is no greater assignment that we have as DBA; without proper adherence to backup and restore practices, our data is completely vulnerable and exposed. This is not an acceptable methodology. To mitigate that risk, we need to prepare for the inevitable, and the best way to do that is to have a solid backup and Restore plan in place.

Differential backups reduce risk by simplifying the backup chain. Every time you execute a differential backup, you remove the need for all transaction log backups taken between the time the last full was taken and the time the differential was taken. Every file that is required for a restore in order to bring a database back online is another opportunity for something to go wrong.

Scenario Without Differential Backups

Let's review a scenario where you do not have differential backups in place. In this scenario, you are a DBA in an environment that has a maximum data loss acceptance of 30 minutes. The easiest way to handle this is to set up a transactional log backup (covered in detail in Chapter 3) that occurs every 30 minutes after a nightly full, as shown in Figure 2-1.

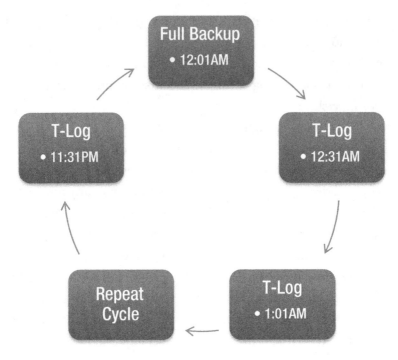

Figure 2-1. *Backup strategy without differential backups*

Continuing with the preceding scenario, imagine the database server crashed at 11:47 PM after the last transaction log backup completed for the day. After a reboot, the SQL instance is up and running, but you find the database is in an unrecoverable state and the only option left is to recover the database from a backup. Easy enough, right? You first restore the full backup and begin restoring the 47 transaction log backup files. But you hit an error at file number 27, the 1:31 PM backup; it is corrupt and will not restore. This results in more than ten hours of data that is unrecoverable and now lost.

Scenario Running Differential Backups

Now let's review a scenario where you have differential backups in place, using the same scenario as before. With this same scenario in mind, and using differential backups, you setup a transactional log backup (again, covered in detail in Chapter 3) that occurs every 30 minutes after a nightly full. In addition, you add in a differential backup that occurs every three hours, as shown in Figure 2-2.

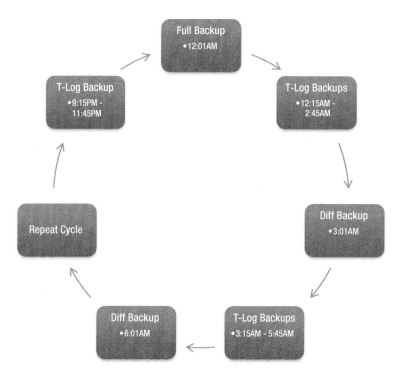

Figure 2-2. *Backup strategy with differential backups*

Following the same scenario, the database server crashed at 11:47 PM after the last transaction log backup completed for the day. After a reboot, the SQL instance is up and running but you find the database is in an unrecoverable state and the only option left is to recover the database from a backup. This time, your job is much easier, you first restore the full backup, then the differential taken at 9:01 PM, and followed by only five transaction log backup files. The outcome results in a completely restored database with only two minutes of lost data. This is due to being able to skip the entire transaction log file prior to the 9:01 PM differential.

This means that the corrupted data was left out, and we are left with a fresh copy of the database, and more importantly, that the database is free from corruption with a much smaller amount of data loss.

Note   We will cover restoring a database in detail in Chapters 5, 6, and 7.

Adding Differential Backups to a Backup Solution

Adding differential backups to an existing backup solution is as easy as adding a single additional step to an existing backup solution. The frequency of the differential backup will depend on a number of factors; examples of such factors include how much your database relies on transactional data, whether these transactions contain changes to data, the frequency of your transaction log backups, and the frequency of your full backups. As you can see, this is a fairly complex topic, and will be covered in Part III of this book; however, for the sake of simplicity, we will use the scenarios in the previous section as the basis for sample backup strategies highlighting the difference between having differential backups in a backup solution. Table 2-1 shows the breakdown of a simple backup strategy without differentials, and Table 2-2 shows the same time frame with differentials.

Table 2-1. *Sample Backup Strategy without Differentials*

	Start Time	**Frequency**	**Total Files (24 hours)**
Full Backup	Every 24 hours	Every 24 hours	1
T-Log Backup	12:30 AM	Every 30 minutes	47

Table 2-2. *Sample Backup Strategy with Differentials*

	Start Time	Frequency	Total Files (24 hours)
Full Backup	Every 24 hours	Every 24 hours	1
Diff Backup	3:01 AM	Every 3 hours	7
T-Log Backup	12:15 AM	Every 30 minutes	48

As I stressed previously, adding differential backups to a backup strategy reduces risk at the expense of disk space. Let's look at some file and data loss comparisons using the two preceding solutions.

Table 2-3 shows a comparison of the two basic backup solutions detailed previously. This figure compares the number of files required to restore the database to the latest point in time possible, in addition to giving the amount of data loss in minutes.

Table 2-3. *Required Files for Restore*

Differential Backups without Differentials

Outage Time	Full File(s)	Diff File(s)	T-Log File(s)	Total Files	Data Loss (m)
2:00 AM	1	0	3	4	29
6:00 AM	1	0	11	12	29
12:30 PM	1	0	24	25	29
11:57 PM	1	0	47	48	26

Differential Backups with Differentials

Outage Time	Full File(s)	Diff File(s)	T-Log File(s)	Total Files	Data Loss (m)
2:00 AM	1	0	4	5	15
6:00 AM	1	1	6	8	15
12:30 PM	1	1	1	3	15
11:57 PM	1	1	6	8	12

As you can see, by adding differentials into the backup solution, the number of files required will never exceed eight (one full, one diff, and six transaction logs). So an outage late in the day would have an 83% reduction in require files for a restore, reducing your overall risk significantly.

It is important to note that if one of the differential backups becomes corrupted at this point, we can still use the transaction logs to restore to the same point in time.

Preparing for a Differential Backup

Continuing to use the database we created in Chapter 1, backrecTestDB, lets prepare for a differential backup. Because this is a test database and has had no data change for quite a while, kicking off a differential backup right now will have very little effect. It would create a 1KB backup file that could be restored; however, for testing purposes, that is not very useful. So instead, let's create a quick script that creates a new table and copies a few rows into it.

The new table can be created by running the following script:

```
SELECT TOP 500000 * INTO [users_DiffTestData]
FROM [users1]
```

When the script completes, you should see the following output:

```
(500000 row(s) affected)
```

Finally, the last thing we want to do is validate that the table we created is correct. Of course, we could have specified the database in the SELECT INTO script; however, for this test, I would rather us check by hand.

In the object viewer panel, right-click the backrecTestDB and select Refresh. Next, expand the database, followed by expanding tables. You should see three tables listed, as shown in Figure 2-3.

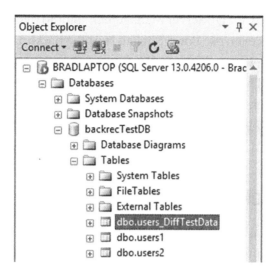

Figure 2-3. *Object Explorer showing tables*

Note   The previous step assumes you followed the steps in Chapter 1: **created the test database**, **built the tables** and **inserted data**, and **took a full backup**. If any of those steps were skipped, you must turn back to Chapter 1 and complete them prior to running the preceding script.

Once this script is complete and we have validated that the new table exists, we are ready to kick off a differential backup.

Running a Differential Backup

Like most things in Microsoft's world, there are numerous ways you can execute a differential backup. If the backup was part of your backup strategy, the execution of the differential backup would be part of the solution (e.g., part of the SQL maintenance plan or a separate stand-alone SQL Server Agent job). If you were manually executing the backup, you could fire it off from within the GUI of SQL Server Management Studio (SSMS), use T-SQL and script it out, or even use PowerShell to start the backup.

In this chapter, I am going to walk you through using the GUI in SSMS and using T-SQL. The end result will be the same in both cases: we will end up with a differential backup that can be restored to the database successfully. Using PowerShell here would be a great idea; however, it is a topic of its own and deserves far more attention than I can give it here.

Taking a Backup via the GUI in SSMS

Taking a differential backup with SSMS via the GUI is identical to taking a full backup. Because of this, I will not go over all the options in the GUI; instead I will cover just the differences required to change the backup from a full to a differential.

A differential backup can be completed in six easy steps:

- Right-click backrecTestDB

- Hover over Tasks and click Back Up...

- On the General screen click, the Backup Type drop-down and select Differential

- Under Destination, click Remove, then Add

- In the File Name text box, enter "E:\SQL Server\ Backup\backrecTestDB_diff.bak" and click OK

- Back on the General tab, click OK

Figure 2-4 shows the backup General tab configured for a differential backup set with the correct configuration.

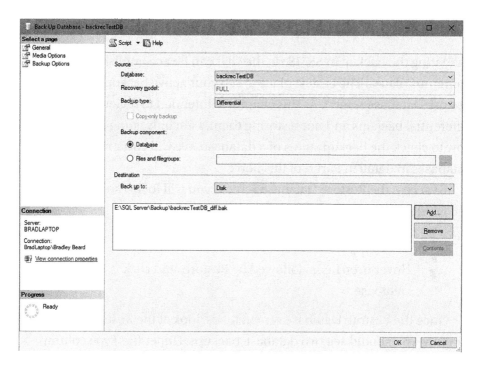

Figure 2-4. *Differential backup settings*

Once the final OK is pressed, you will see a progress percentage on the bottom left of the "Back Up Database" window. Because we only duplicated 500,000 rows into the new table, the backup will complete in a few seconds. A completion window will pop up, confirming that the backup was successful, as in Figure 2-5.

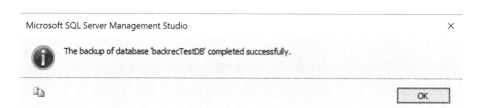

Figure 2-5. *Backup complete window*

Validating a Backup via the GUI in SSMS

Validating the backup in SSMS via the GUI can be accomplished in numerous places. The easiest place to see your active backups is in the Restore Database screen. As this chapter is intended to review executing differential backups and not restoring them, I am only going to skim over how to check the backup status of a database. We will cover restoring databases in detail in Part II of this book.

To access the Restore Database screen, you will follow similar steps you would use to get into the Backup screen.

- Right-click backrecTestDB

- Hover over Tasks, followed by Restore, and click Database

Once the Restore Database screen loads, look at the Restore Plan window: you should see two database backups. Under the Type column, you should see a backup listed as a full and differential, as shown in Figure 2-6.

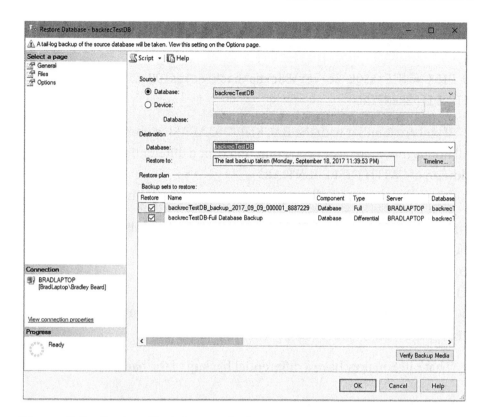

Figure 2-6. *Restore Database window*

This can be considered "proof of life" that the backup proceeded as intended, and is ready for recovery from this interface. Again, we will get into the restoring aspect of this operation later in this book. For now, you can be assured that the backups are ready to be restored though.

Taking a Differential Backup via T-SQL

Executing a differential backup via T-SQL is quite easy. There are a number of arguments that can be passed with the script; however, for this example, we are going to keep this script simple.

In SQL Studio Manager, run the following script:

```
BACKUP DATABASE [backrecTestDB]
TO DISK = N'E:\SQL Server\Backup\backrecTestDB_diff.bak'
WITH DIFFERENTIAL
```

If you are familiar with the BACKUP DATABASE command, you will notice that there is only one difference for a differential backup, the addition of "WITH DIFFERENTIAL."

When the script completes, you will see an output similar to this:

```
Processed 52688 pages for database 'backrecTestDB',
file 'backrecTestDB' on file 1.
Processed 2 pages for database 'backrecTestDB',
file 'backrecTestDB_log' on file 1.
BACKUP DATABASE WITH DIFFERENTIAL successfully processed
52690 pages in 9.620 seconds (42.790 MB/sec).
```

That's it! You now have a differential backup of the backrecTestDB.

Summary

This chapter walked us though the basics of differential backups and why they are important. It showed us how differential backups can reduce overall risk to data recovery by reducing the number of files required for a database recovery.

Chapter 3 will cover transaction logs, the last backup type. Chapter 4 will walk you through setting up a complete backup solution and review in detail the applicable industry standards or best practices regarding backups.

After Chapter 4 is complete, Part I will be complete as well. At that point, you should have a cursory understanding of how the different parts of the backup work, together and separately. We will then use that knowledge to build the second part of the backup/restore procedure in Part II, where we focus on restoring data that has been backed up. Finally, Part III will have us tie the parts together into one interface, and then automate it using SQL Server Agent.

CHAPTER 3

Transaction Log Backups

In this chapter, we will be focusing on the different techniques behind backing up transaction logs. This is the last piece of the puzzle as far as a complete backup solution, which consists of full, differential, and transaction log backups. This particular piece is important because, without transaction log backups, there can be no point-in-time restorations. In fact, there can be no restorations beyond what was in the last differential backup, and any data committed to the database since the last differential backup will be permanently lost since this data is resident only in the transaction log. For this reason, transaction logs are often viewed as the single most important piece of disaster recovery since they provide the missing pieces of data since the last differential backup.

Without the transaction log backups, we would not be able to perform any backups outside of full or differential backups (not taking into account the backup types not discussed in this book, including file and filegroup backups, mirror backups, partial backups, and copy-only backups). While this may not seem too bad, it is important to remember that the transaction log must be backed up regularly in order to keep the database running optimally.

© Bradley Beard 2018
B. Beard, *Beginning Backup and Restore for SQL Server*,
https://doi.org/10.1007/978-1-4842-3456-3_3

What Is a Transaction Log?

The transaction log is a file that contains a log of all of the changed or updated data from all database transactions. Every time the database state changes because of a modification to the data, the interaction with the database is kept in a log. The transactions in the log are written in the order they are received, so the transactions are all sequential. With this in mind, it is possible to "rewind" the state of the database transaction by transaction according to a specific timeframe, until reaching the desired state. This is known as a point-in-time restore.

Note   A point-in-time restore can be extremely time-consuming, but the advantage is that the granularity of the transaction log is such that individual transactions can be targeted to achieve the desired results.

Transaction logs also have the unique characteristic of growing extremely large over a relatively short period of time. For example, once a differential backup is run, that backup does not continue to grow. Similarly, a transaction log will continue to grow until it is backed up. These transaction log backups will then continue in the specified backup intervals for as long as there is disk space or until they are turned off. Each of these transaction logs will be able to restore to the last differential backup, and they cannot restore to any other backup. For this reason, all of the backups—full, differential, and transaction log—must be functioning 100% correctly in order for there to be the minimal amount of data loss. Without verifying that our transaction log backups are running correctly, the transaction log, over time, will eventually take over the entire disk. Obviously, allowing a transaction log to take over the entirety of a storage volume is not what anyone would call an ideal solution, and for that reason, we need to ensure that our backups are running smoothly and correctly. To help facilitate that goal, the next section will show us how to properly view the status of the transaction logs resident in SQL Server.

Viewing Transaction Log Status

There are a few different ways that you can view the status, or size, of the transaction log for each database in your system. The most common way of viewing the status is to run a simple query. Open up a new query in SSMS and type in this query:

```
DBCC SQLPERF(LOGSPACE);
```

Running that query will return what is shown in Figure 3-1.

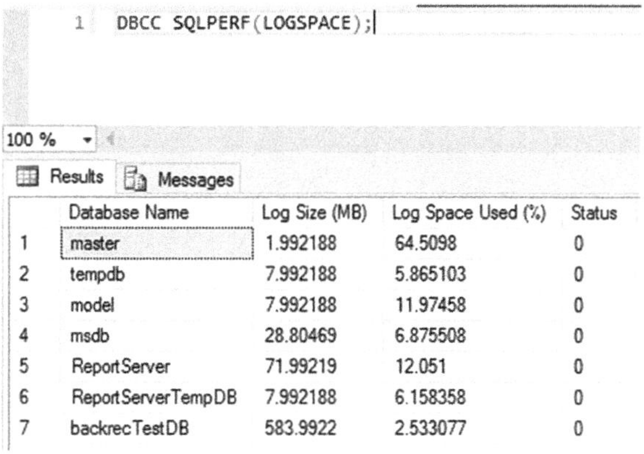

	Database Name	Log Size (MB)	Log Space Used (%)	Status
1	master	1.992188	64.5098	0
2	tempdb	7.992188	5.865103	0
3	model	7.992188	11.97458	0
4	msdb	28.80469	6.875508	0
5	ReportServer	71.99219	12.051	0
6	ReportServerTempDB	7.992188	6.158358	0
7	backrecTestDB	583.9922	2.533077	0

Figure 3-1. *SQLPERF results*

The columns returned from this query are as follows:

- Database Name: the name of the database being analyzed

- Log Size (MB): the size of the transaction log

- Log Space Used (%): percentage of allocated space being used by the log

- Status: this column always returns 0

Another way to view the current size of the transaction log is to right-click the database name in SSMS and select Properties, and then choose Files from the left menu. A screen opens, which is shown in Figure 3-2.

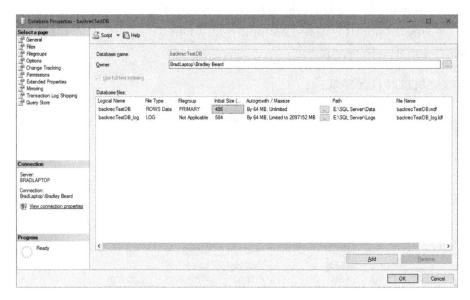

Figure 3-2. *Files options*

From here, we can see that the Initial Size column is the same size as the value from the query in Figure 3-1. This is because I have not yet backed up my transaction log, so the initial size is shown to be the current value. Once I back up the log, I will be able to go back to this screen and see a much smaller initial value.

Consequently, we could also just look in the file system for an approximation of size for the transaction log. Simply navigate to where you are saving your logs (E:\SQL Server\Logs for me) and you should see something similar to what is shown in Figure 3-3.

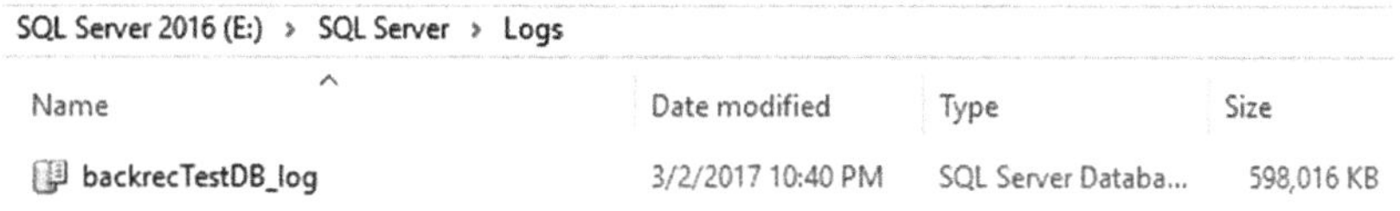

SQL Server 2016 (E:) › SQL Server › Logs			
Name ^	Date modified	Type	Size
🗐 backrecTestDB_log	3/2/2017 10:40 PM	SQL Server Databa...	598,016 KB

Figure 3-3. *File system view*

Like I said, that's more of an approximation because there is some overhead in the file size, as you can see.

Recall that the purpose of a backup, whether a full, differential, or transaction log, is to be able to restore data to a previous state. At its most basic level, a proper backup strategy is accomplished through the following steps:

- Planning a backup strategy

- Implementing the backup strategy

- Verifying the backup strategy

In other words, first you must plan the strategy for the backup by determining what level of data availability you would like. Then, you must implement that strategy in SQL Server. Finally, you must verify that the backup strategy is functioning correctly and that the backups can be restored as expected in the case of emergency.

In the case of transaction log backups, the principle of verification becomes highlighted somewhat more than in full or differential backups, because the transaction log is the key to disaster recovery. For this reason, I personally tend to focus slightly more on transaction logs than on full or differential backups. Not to diminish the importance of the full or differential backups at all, but the transaction log, being the literal log of transactions in the database, seems much more important in my mind.

Backing Up a Transaction Log

As to be expected, there are a few ways that we can run backups of the transaction log: either by writing a custom SQL script, or by using the familiar SSMS interface. In this section, I will detail the different pieces of each of these two scenarios, and leave it as an exercise to the student to decide which method works for their particular application. What is important to remember is that these techniques can be used either as part of a maintenance plan or as bespoke methods to provide a heightened level of data security. I will always recommend using SQL Server Agent to manage your backups through the use of a properly planned and managed maintenance plan though.

Figure 3-2 showed the initial size of the transaction log as 584MB. After a regularly scheduled transaction log backup, the initial size is now 24MB, as shown in Figure 3-4.

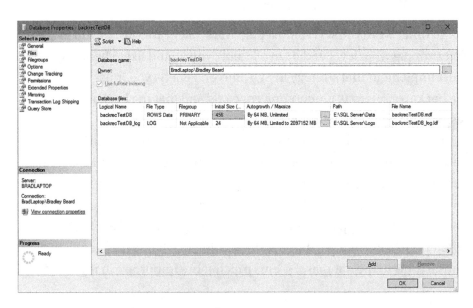

Figure 3-4. *Initial size changed*

Let's look at the different ways of getting our transaction log backed up.

Transaction Log Backups via Script

If we didn't have a backup scheduled in a maintenance plan, or even if we did and we just wanted another backup of the transaction log, we could have run a backup of the transaction log manually by using the following script:

```
BACKUP LOG backrecTestDB
TO DISK = 'E:\SQL Server\Logs\backrecTestDB.trn'
```

Just fill in your database name in the first and last parts of that script, and you can issue your own backup command manually. This script is particularly useful if you ever come across an issue where the transaction log has somehow filled up before it has been scheduled to back up automatically.

With this script, there are attributes that can be added after TO DISK. Those are

- WITH PASSWORD = 'password'

  - Replace password with a password of your choice. This password must be entered in order to restore this backup.

- WITH STATS = X

  - Replace X with an integer of your choice. This is the interval in percent that has been completed. For example, WITH STATS = 5 will show progress after every 5% of completion.

- WITH DESCRIPTION = 'text'

  - Replace text with whatever you want the description to be.

Transaction Log Backups via SSMS

Backing up the transaction log via SSMS is a bit more involved of a process, but ultimately gives us the same result. There isn't a major fundamental difference in these methods, since they accomplish the same goal of a transaction log backup, so it really is going to come down to what you prefer and what is ideal for your environment according to any business rules you have in place.

To start a transaction log backup in SSMS, first you need to right-click the database name and hover on Tasks, and drill down into the Backup option, as shown in Figure 3-5.

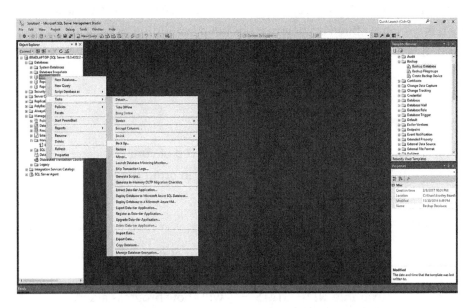

Figure 3-5. *Back Up option*

The initial screen, as shown in Figure 3-6, is titled General. There are two more options on this page in the left-hand menu titled Media Options and Backup Options. Let's take a quick look at these menu options and what choices they have within their respective areas.

Back Up Database—General

Selecting this menu option opens up the General page of the Back Up Database window, as shown in Figure 3-6.

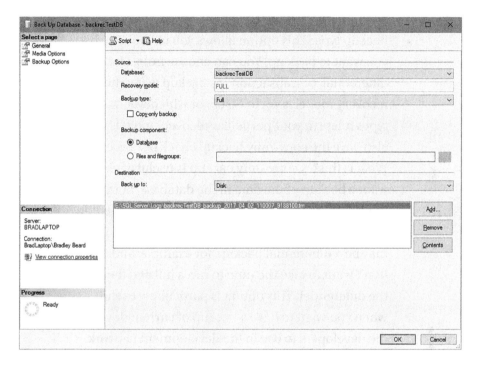

Figure 3-6. *General window*

This interface allows us to define the various "general" pieces of the puzzle for transaction log backups. The options available here are

- Source

  - Database: This option allows you to choose which database you would like to back up from your available databases.

- Recovery model: This option will always default to the recovery model currently in use by the selected database. To test this, select the `master` database and you will see the recovery model change from FULL to SIMPLE.

- Backup type: This option allows you to choose what you want to back up. You can choose from a full, differential, or transaction log backup when the recovery model is set to FULL, or whichever backup types relate to your particular recovery model. You also have the copy-only backup check box here. What is this? A copy-only backup is useful when you want a backup of the data in the database, but you don't want to interrupt the normal backup schedule and you also don't want to use the latest backup; it may be a differential backup, for example, and you don't want to take the time to run a full and then the differential. This option is particularly useful when you want to have a backup of current data for the developers to use in the development network. Think of it as an out-of-sequence complete backup.

- Backup component

  - Database

  - Files and filegroups

- Destination

  - Back up to: The options in this area are currently disk or URL. Select the disk option to save the backup in a physical drive somewhere on your connected network, and use the URL option to save to an online storage system or an Azure instance. Choosing one of these options gives you the ability to select the location by clicking the Add or Remove buttons on the bottom right-hand side of this window.

For this example, we want to choose transaction log from the *Backup type* drop-down menu before moving to the Media Options submenu. The final state of the interface is shown in Figure 3-7.

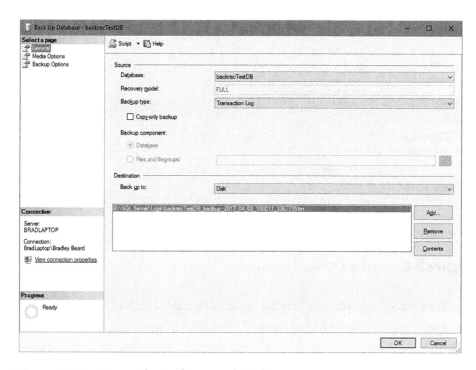

Figure 3-7. *General window, updated*

Back Up Database—Media Options

Choosing this option will show the following interface, as shown in Figure 3-8.

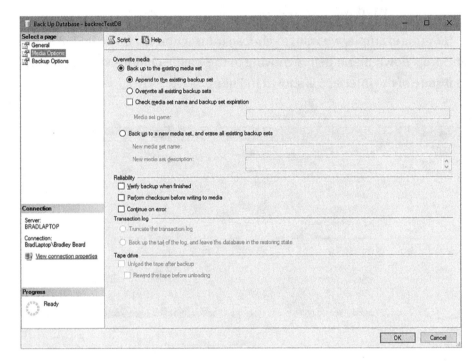

Figure 3-8. *Media Options window*

This screen lets you choose the options that deal with how the physical storage of the backup is to be handled. Included in this screen are the following options:

- Overwrite media

    - Back up to the existing media set: This option lets you add a backup to an existing backup, which will then let you decide which backup want to restore, in the case of restoration.

- Append to the existing backup set: If you want to add it to the set as mentioned in the preceding, select this option.

- Overwrite all existing backup sets: If you would rather overwrite the selected backup set with the new backup you are about to run, select this option.

- Check media set name and backup set expiration: This isn't necessary, and isn't used often in my experience, but it can be selected if you want to verify the name and expiration of the backup set.

- Media set name

- Back up to a new media set, and erase all existing backup sets: This is different from the previous option. The previous option would back up to the existing backup set; this option lets you create an entirely new backup set, and then save the backup to that backup set. Also, this option deletes any previous backup sets, so use this option carefully.

  - New media set name: The name of the new backup set.

  - New media set description: An optional description of the backup set.

- Reliability

  - Verify backup when finished

  - Perform checksum before writing to media

  - Continue on error

- Transaction log

    - Truncate the transaction log

    - Back up the tail of the log, and leave the database in the restoring state

- Tape drive

    - Unload the tape after backup

    - Rewind the tape before unloading

Let's stop for a moment and go over the differences between the two transaction log options just introduced. When referencing the backup of a transaction log, two things are important: the transaction log can be truncated, or the tail of the transaction log can be backed up. So what's the difference?

The first option, *Truncate the transaction log*, deals specifically with truncating the log and that's it. Truncating the transaction log does not reduce the size of the physical transaction log file. This concept seemed counterintuitive to me at first, but then I realized that in order to reduce the size of the log file, you have to shrink the log file. Truncation simply removes the parts of the log file that aren't being used; shrinking the log file is what actually makes the log smaller. Also important to remember is that truncation automatically happens after a checkpoint (in the simple recovery model) and after a log backup (in the full or bulk-logged recovery model). This means that truncation will automatically happen as part of the regular backup procedure, if a procedure has been properly established. If a procedure has not been properly established, then your transaction log will never be truncated (unless manually) and will eventually grow to the entire size of the storage media.

The second option, *Back up the tail of the log, and leave the database in the restoring state*, is the more robust and useful of the two options. This option allows you to back up the latest transactions that haven't been backed up, and then leave the database ready to immediately restore, if necessary. This is known as the *tail-log backup*.

For the purpose of this example, make sure that this first option, *Truncate the transaction log*, is selected, along with *Verify backup when finished*.

The final interface is shown in Figure 3-9.

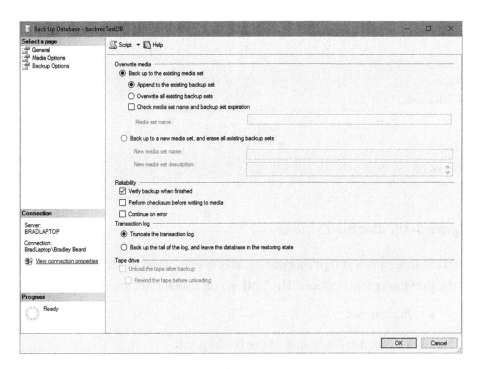

Figure 3-9. *Media Options window, updated*

Back Up Database—Backup Options

Choosing this option will show the following interface, as shown in Figure 3-10.

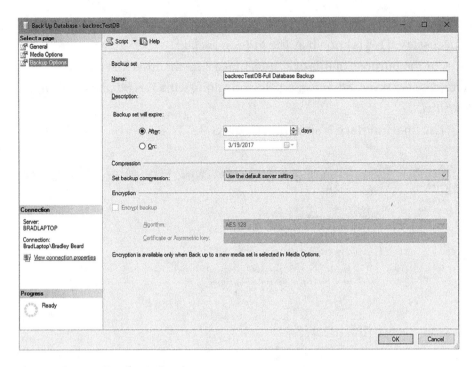

Figure 3-10. *Backup Options*

This screen lets you define the actual criteria of the media sets defined in the previous menu option. The options on this screen are

- Backup set

    - Name: The name of the backup set.

    - Description: The optional description of the backup set.

    - Backup set will expire:

        - After: The number of days that the backup will stay "fresh"; after this value has passed, the backup expires and is no longer valid.

        - On: The date that the data expires.

- Compression

  - Set backup compression: If you want to compress the backup, choose this option. Compression is not necessary in all cases, but is generally a good idea just to save on space constraints when you are dealing with very large databases. Note that compression is only available on SQL Server 2016 Enterprise, Standard, and Developer versions.

- Encryption

  - Encrypt backup

    - Algorithm

    - Certificate or asymmetric key

We aren't going to change anything on this screen, since these default options are what we need. Note that the Encryption option is only available when the *Back up to a new media set* option is selected in the *Media Options* submenu. This is also explained on the actual interface shown in Figure 3-8.

Once you get to this final screen and are ready to begin your backup, click the OK button. Hopefully, you will see a window which opens after a very short time and explains that the backup was successful. This window is shown in Figure 3-11.

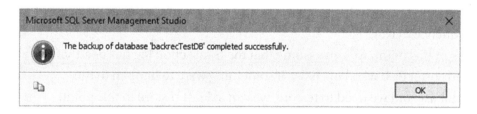

Figure 3-11. *Backup successful*

When I view the properties on the created backup file, I see what is shown in Figure 3-12.

Figure 3-12. *Transaction log properties*

The fields I want to check are the Created and Modified fields. Created shows that the file was created 50 minutes ago; that is correct, because the time I ran this backup was 11:50 AM, and the log was created at 11:00 AM as part of my regular backup sequence. It was modified 3 minutes ago, which was when the backed-up log was added to the current backup set. We could also look at the size of the backup, and estimate that it should be roughly twice as big since it is nearly time for the automated backup sequence to run.

At this point, we can assume that the transaction log has been safely and correctly backed up. Now, if something were to happen to the database and we need to restore, we can at least restore to this point, considering that we have the differential and full backups. From a transaction log point of view, we are all set up though.

Summary

In this chapter, we learned a bit about what transaction logs are, how they work, how they relate to the database, and how to actually back them up from script and from a GUI. In the next chapter, I will tie these first three chapters together into a complete solution for backing up a database.

CHAPTER 4

Backup Solution Examples

This chapter is going to serve as the culmination of Chapter 1 (on full backups), Chapter 2 (on differential backups), and Chapter 3 (on transaction log backups). We will first get into the creation of a sustainable maintenance plan to manage our backups all together in one main area using a set schedule, as opposed to manually running backups or having full, differential, or transaction log backups running at different times, and then we will run that plan and review.

Setting Up the Maintenance Plan

In order to automate the backups, we need to have SQL Server Agent aware of the routines that need to be run, and when to run them. This is accomplished through the use of maintenance plans. Every aspect of an automated backup plan can be configured within a maintenance plan, so let's step through the various inner workings of a solid backup plan.

Full Backup Configuration

To start, go to SSMS and expand the *Management* node. Next, right-click *Maintenance Plans* and choose *Maintenance Plan Wizard*. The first interface we see is titled Select Plan Properties. Enter a name of Backup

© Bradley Beard 2018
B. Beard, *Beginning Backup and Restore for SQL Server*,
https://doi.org/10.1007/978-1-4842-3456-3_4

Maintenance Plan in the Name box, and a brief description as well. Click the radio button for *Separate schedules for each task* also. Figure 4-1 shows what you should see. When you are ready, click Next to continue.

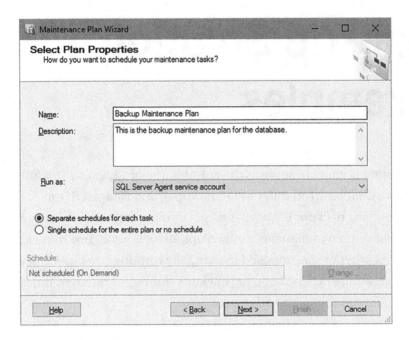

Figure 4-1. *Select Plan Properties*

The next screen lets us select which maintenance tasks we want to run in this plan. We want to choose the three tasks related to backups: specifically, *Back Up Database (Full)*, *Back Up Database (Differential)*, and *Back Up Database (Transaction Log)*. These selections are shown as part of Figure 4-2.

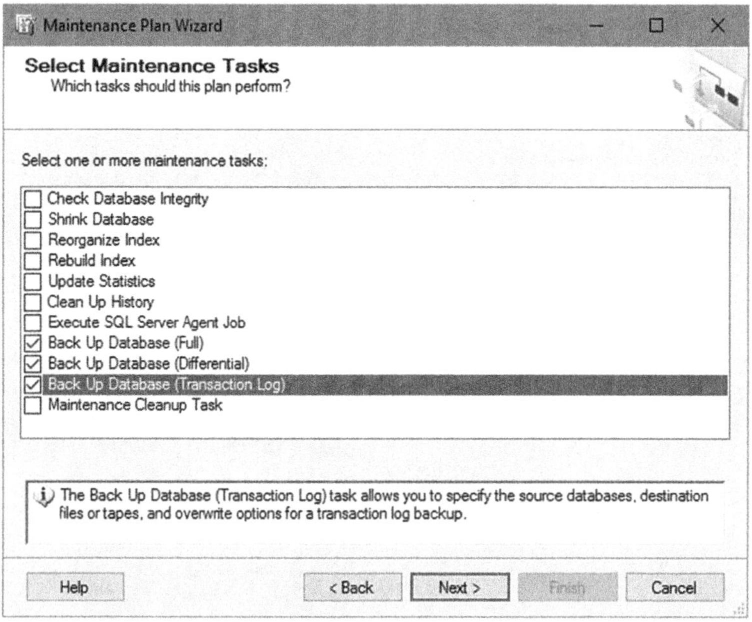

Figure 4-2. *Select Maintenance Tasks*

Now, click Next and we will choose the order of the three parts of the backup, as shown in Figure 4-3. Since we are going to be executing these on different schedules and not chaining them together in the same plan (i.e., we are not going to run all three at the same time under the heading of full, differential, or transaction log), we can bypass this page. Click the Next button when you are ready to proceed.

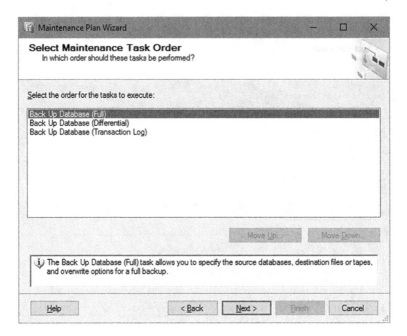

Figure 4-3. *Select Maintenance Task*

Because we left the default order in place on the previous screen, the first interface that comes up is the *Define Back Up Database (Full) Task* screen. There are three tabs on this screen titled General, Destination, and Options, with the default screen being General. Figure 4-4 shows this initial interface.

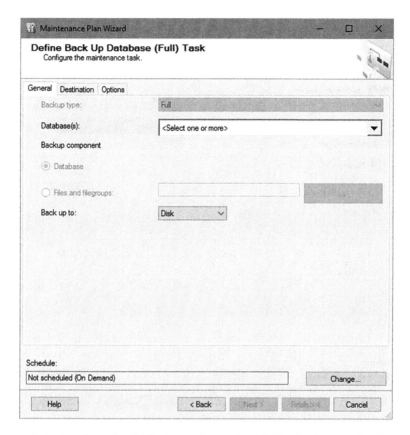

Figure 4-4. *Define Back Up Database (Full) Task, General tab*

Pull down the Database(s) menu and select the databases you would like to back up. It can be any database you like, as long as it has been set up with the full recovery model. Once a database is selected, Figure 4-5 shows what should be seen in the main screen.

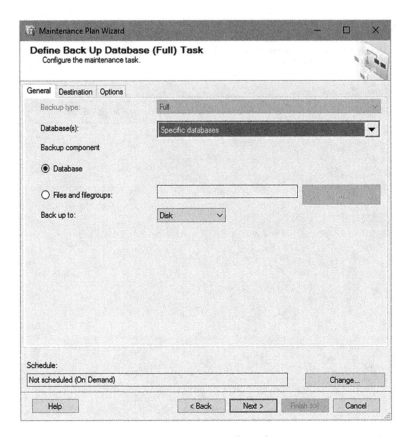

Figure 4-5. *Define Back Up Database (Full) Task, General tab (updated)*

Note that the *Database* radio button is now selected. This is because a database has been detected and is now the subject of this task. Consequently, you could also choose the *Files and filegroups* radio button if you want to run backups of individual files.

On this screen, there is also an option labeled *Back up to:* that is new for SQL Server 2016. Previously, we did not have the option to back up to a URL, but we do now, thanks to the innovations that Microsoft has made with the integration of SQL Server into cloud-based infrastructure such as Microsoft Azure. Getting into the specifics of Azure is out of the scope of this book, but this is a fantastic addition to an already powerful platform. For most purposes, this can be kept at Disk, although it can change for your particular situation.

The bottom of this screen has the Schedule option. We won't worry about this until we have set all of the options in the three different tabs first, so don't worry about that just yet. Click the Destination tab when you are ready to continue.

Figure 4-6 shows the initial view of the Destination tab. This tab lets us define where the backups should be stored.

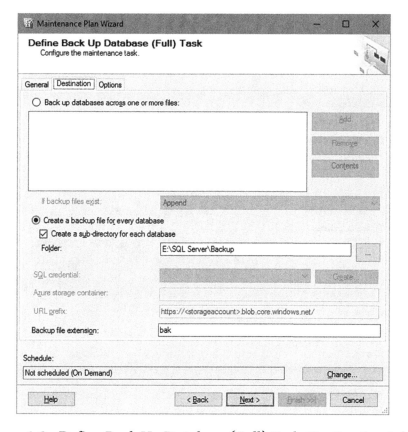

Figure 4-6. *Define Back Up Database (Full) Task, Destination tab*

It is important to note that this interface changes depending on the selection of the *Back up to:* field in the General tab.

Notice the radio button labeled *Create a backup file for every database.* Since we are using this specifically for configuring the setting for a full backup of the database, click the check box under this option for *Create a sub-directory for each database.* This means that, for every database you choose to back up, those backups are going to be kept in a directory with the name of the database as the name of the directory.

When you're ready to move on, click the Options tab. Figure 4-7 will be what you see next.

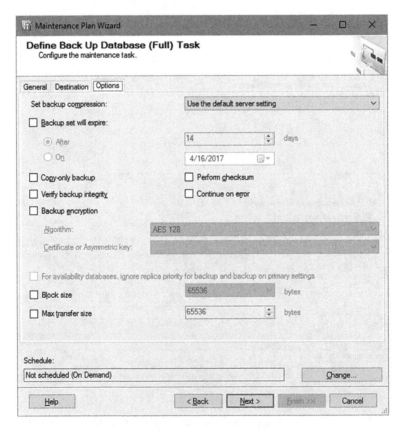

Figure 4-7. *Define Back Up Database (Full) Task, Options tab*

This is where we can set the other various settings for the task. From the figure, you can see that we have options for compression, backup expiration, and encryption. For this demonstration, we are going to keep these options just as they are without compression or encryption. The only thing I want to change on this screen is to check the check box for *Verify backup integrity*. This isn't 100% necessary if your database has already had integrity checks run against it, but just in case, I want to make sure that this option is selected. Better safe than sorry, especially when you are on the receiving end of a failed backup that might have been avoided if this option were selected.

At the bottom of the screen, click the *Change...* button to set up the schedule for this task.

Let's take a minute and define what our backup schedule should look like and when it should run. Let's assume that we want our backups to run in a 24-hour window, so there is minimal interruption of data. If the full backup is set at midnight, then the first differential would be set at midnight also, followed by the first transaction log backup as well. Then every six hours, a new differential backup will run. Inside of those, transaction log backups will run every hour. Table 4-1 is a fairly accurate representation of the time block I am describing.

Table 4-1. *24-Hour Backup Schedule Example*

Time	Full?	Differential?	Transaction Log?
12:00 AM	X	X	X
1:00 AM			X
2:00 AM			X
3:00 AM			X
4:00 AM			X
5:00 AM			X

(*continued*)

Table 4-1. (*continued*)

Time	Full?	Differential?	Transaction Log?
6:00 AM		X	X
7:00 AM			X
8:00 AM			X
9:00 AM			X
10:00 AM			X
11:00 AM			X
12:00 PM		X	X
1:00 PM			X
2:00 PM			X
3:00 PM			X
4:00 PM			X
5:00 PM			X
6:00 PM		X	X
7:00 PM			X
8:00 PM			X
9:00 PM			X
10:00 PM			X
11:00 PM			X

Using this model, we can restore to any hour in a given day, meaning that the most data we will lose is 1 hour. If this is acceptable, we can move on. If not, then we can adjust the time between backups. We will stay with this schedule for now though. Figure 4-8 shows what the updated interface should look like.

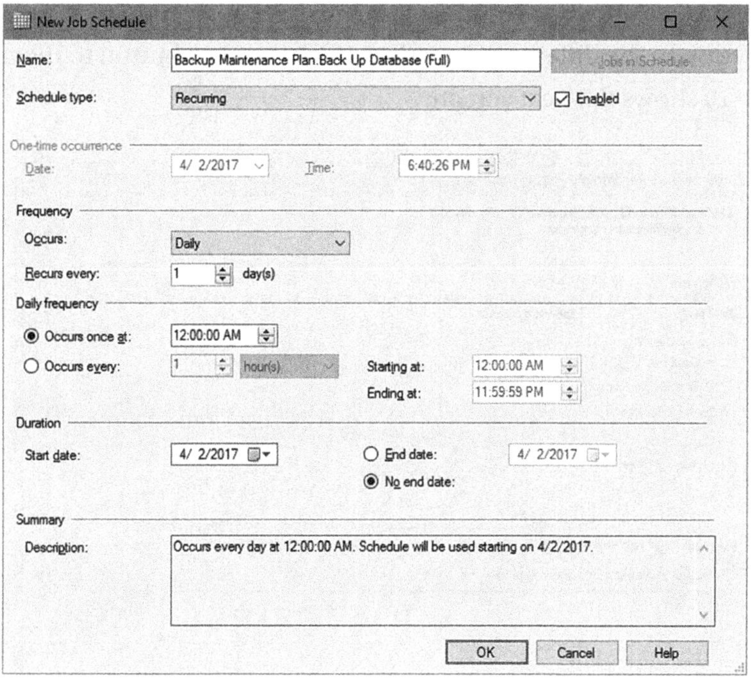

Figure 4-8. *New Job Schedule*

All you need to do is to pull down the Occurs menu and choose Daily.
That's it. Notice the text in the Summary field now reads Occurs every day
at 12:00:00 AM. Schedule will be used starting on [DATE]. Click OK here
to save this schedule, and notice that the same summary we just read
has been transferred to the Schedule block on the interface, as shown in
Figure 4-9.

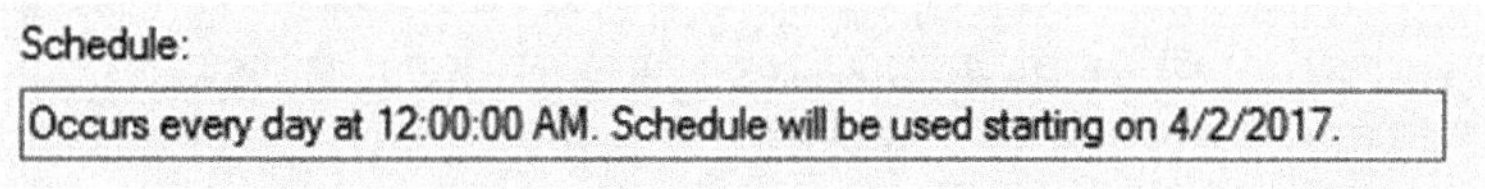

Figure 4-9. *Updated schedule information*

Now that we are done setting up the full backup portion of the plan, let's move on to the differential portion. Click the Next button to move on. Figure 4-10 shows the next screen.

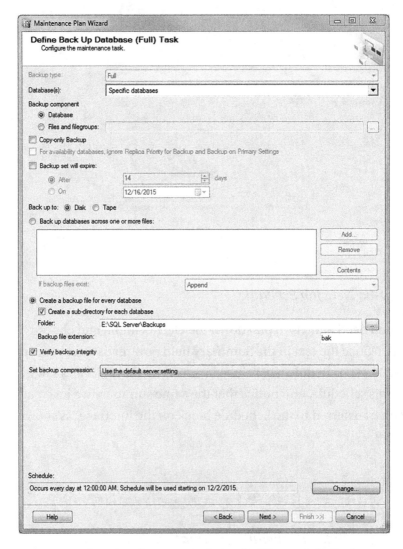

Figure 4-10. *Define Back Up Database (Differential) Task*

Click Next to continue setting up the plan.

Differential Backup Configuration

Next, the Define Back Up Database (Differential) Task interface is displayed. Figure 4-11 shows that the initial interface is nearly exactly like the previous interface, complete with the same three tabs for different menu options. The first tab that we are on now is titled General, so let's look at those options now.

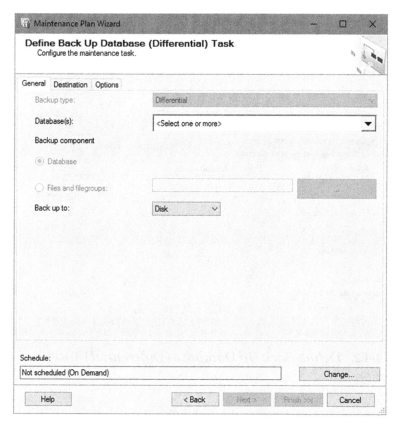

Figure 4-11. Define Back Up Database (Differential) Task, General tab

Just like we did for the full backup section, we are going to choose our database from the drop-down menu labeled *Database(s)*, and click the Destination tab. Figure 4-12 shows the initial view of this tab.

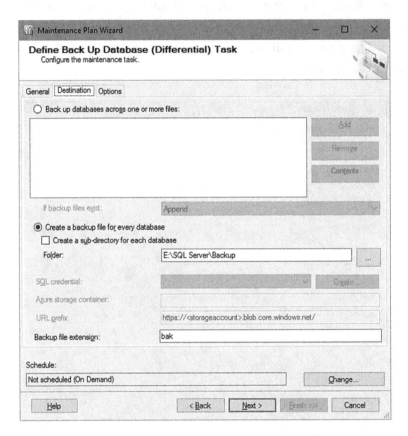

Figure 4-12. *Define Back Up Database (Differential) Task, Destination tab*

Remember that we need to check the *Create a sub-directory for each database* check box before moving on. Also note that the backup location is set to our default backup location, which was originally defined when I installed SQL Server.

Clicking the Options tab shows you what is shown in Figure 4-13. Again, this is identical to what was originally seen. Just be sure to check the *Verify backup integrity* check box before moving on.

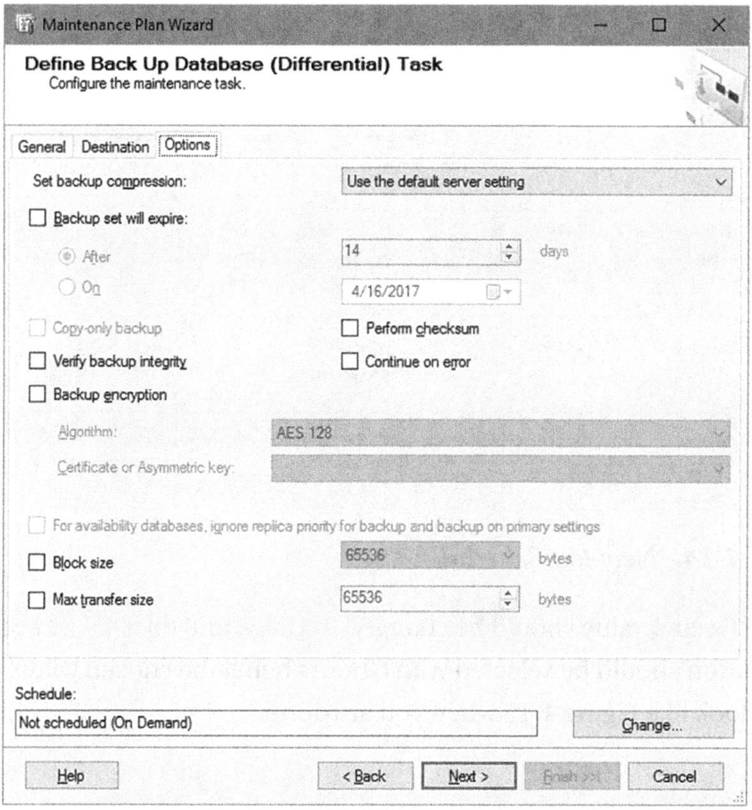

Figure 4-13. *Define Back Up Database (Differential) Task, Options tab*

Once everything looks good, you want to click the Change... button on the bottom of this screen so that we can define the schedule for this task. Figure 4-14 shows the initial interface for the schedule.

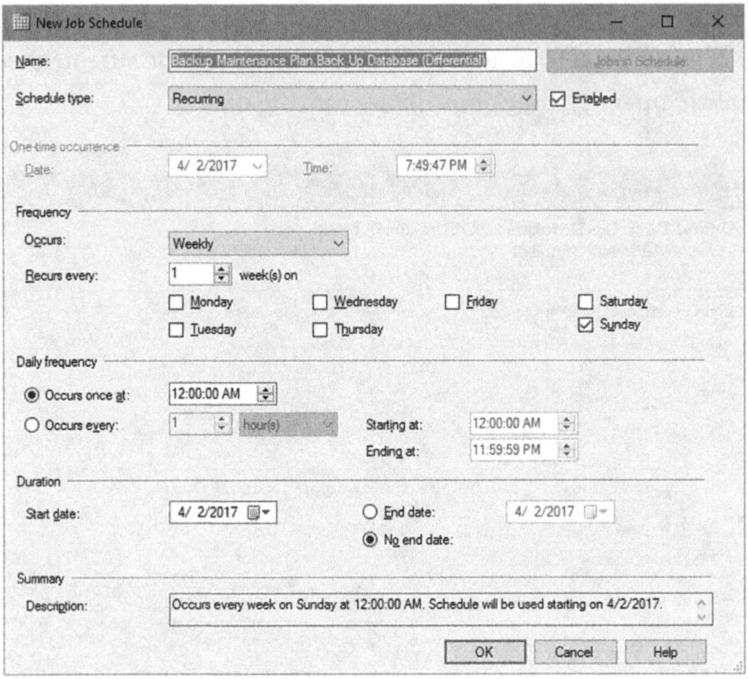

Figure 4-14. *New Job Schedule*

The Occurs value should be changed to Daily, and the Occurs every radio button should be selected with 6 hours being the chosen value. It should look like Figure 4-15 when you are done.

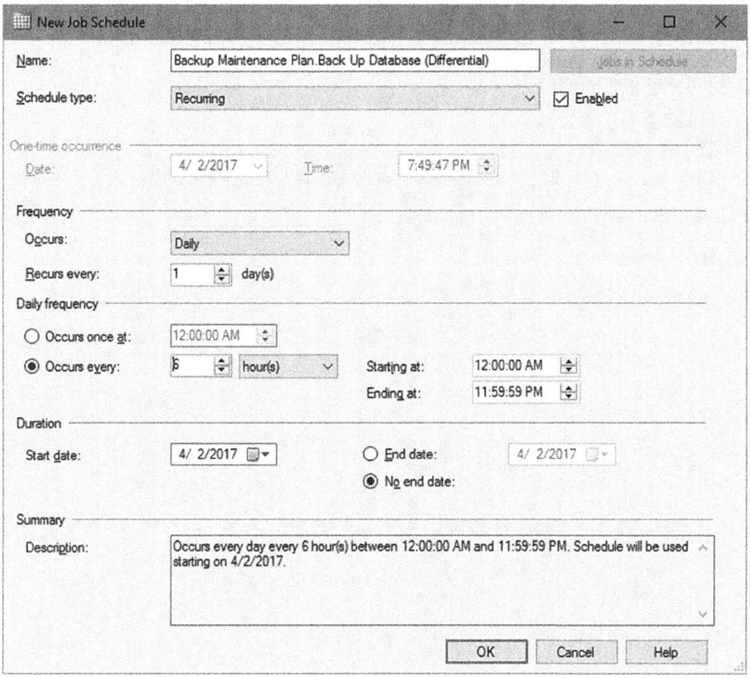

Figure 4-15.   *New Job Schedule, updated*

This means that our differential backup will now run every six hours every day. Click OK when you are done, and then click Next.

Transaction Log Backup Configuration

The next screen that opens up is the Define Back Up Database (Transaction Log) Task screen, as shown in Figure 4-16.

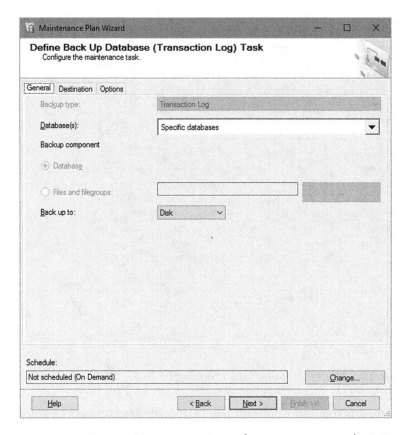

Figure 4-16. *Define Back Up Database (Transaction Log) Task, General tab*

This area has the same basic setting as the two previous General tabs: pick the database from the *Database(s)* menu and ensure that Disk is selected in the *Back up to:* drop-down menu. Notice that, in this interface, the Database radio button is disabled? This is because we aren't backing up the database, but we are backing up the transaction log. On the other interfaces, this option was selectable, and you could choose between backing up the database or the files and filegroups.

Click the Destination tab when you are done, and you should then see what is shown in Figure 4-17.

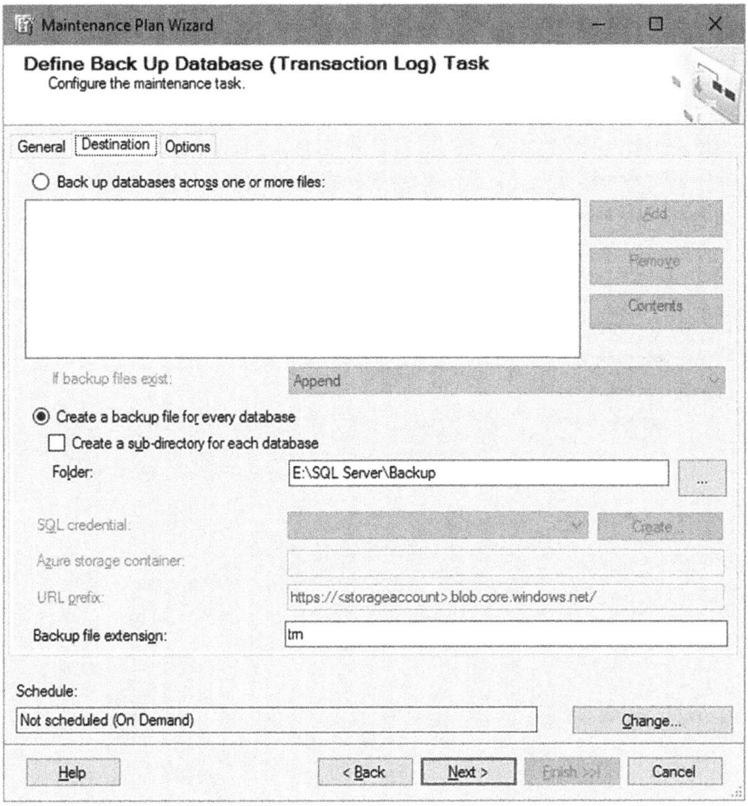

Figure 4-17. *Define Back Up Database (Transaction Log) Task, Destination tab*

Make sure that the *Create a sub-directory for each database* option is checked, and this screen is done. Click the Options tab when you're ready, and Figure 4-18 will be shown.

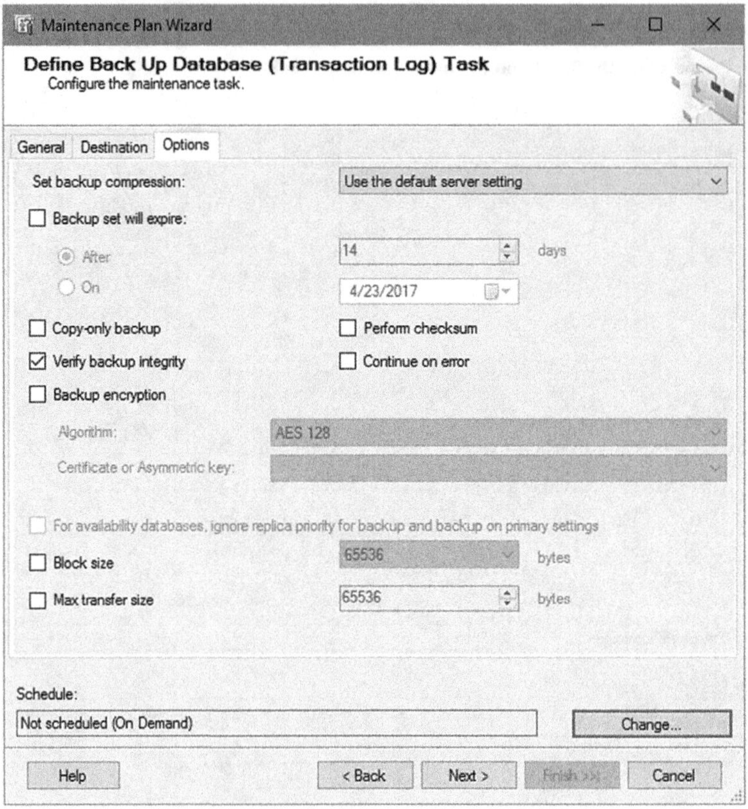

Figure 4-18. *Define Back Up Database (Transaction Log) Task, Options tab*

Ensure that the *Verify backup integrity* check box is checked here, and click the Change... button at the bottom of the screen so we can set up our schedule for transaction log backups. Figure 4-19 shows what your screen should look like after updating the schedule.

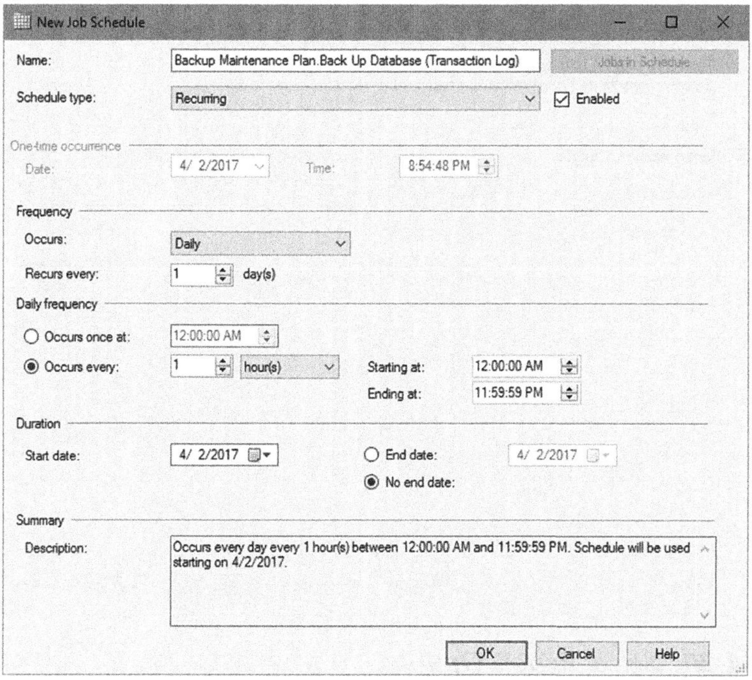

Figure 4-19. *New Job Schedule*

When you are ready to move on, click the OK button to close the Schedule window, and then click the Next button on the interface.

Next comes the screen shown in Figure 4-20, Select Report Options.

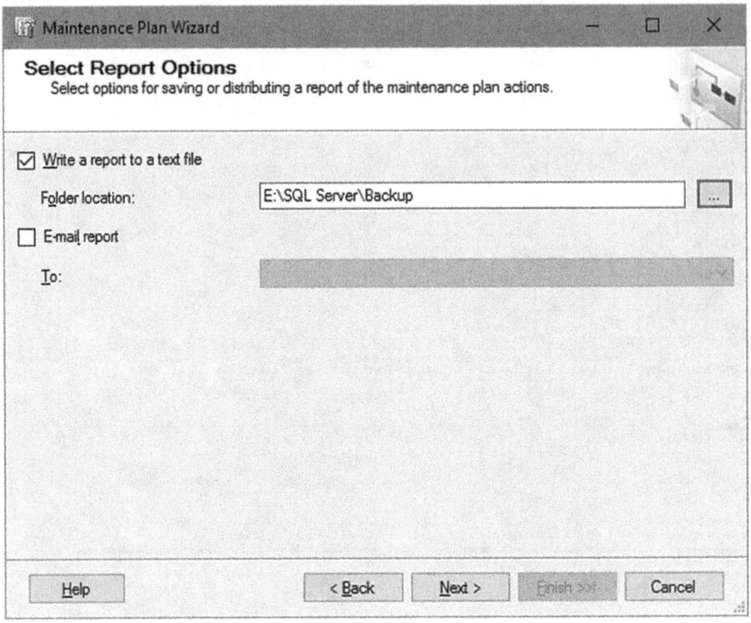

Figure 4-20. *Select Report Options*

Now, this is fairly self-explanatory. If you want a report written to text file and popped into the file system, click the box. Notice that I have chosen the Backup directory, and not the Logs directory? This is because I want to keep the Logs directory for my transaction logs. The Backup directory can be used to store the maintenance text files, while the individual folders inside of the Backup directory will store the actual .bak files in case we ever need to restore the database.

You can also get the report e-mailed to you, but you have to have an Operator defined. If you have an Operator defined, select it here to receive the e-mail. This will let you know, by e-mail, when the maintenance plan runs and what the result was. For now, we will leave only the report selection. Click Next to move on.

On the screen shown in Figure 4-21, titled Complete the Wizard, you will see a summary of what we did. Expanding the options in the interface will show the complete details of what we did, as shown in Figure 4-21.

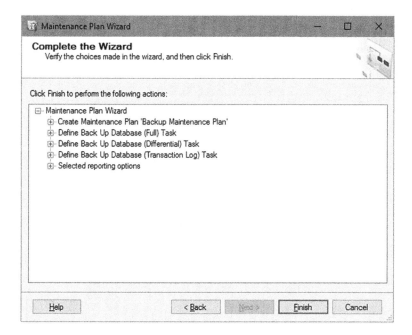

Figure 4-21. *Complete the Wizard*

Note that these options have not been saved yet. You could click
Cancel right here and destroy all of the work we did thus far, but let's not
do that. Instead, review what we did and, when you're ready, click Finish.
Figure 4-22 shows what you should see as the maintenance plan is being
created.

Figure 4-22. *Maintenance Plan Wizard Progress*

Always a good sign! Click Close when you are ready, and notice that Backup Maintenance Plan now appears in the Maintenance Plans area of SSMS. It is now enabled, and will run on the schedule we defined.

Configuring the Jobs

Notice that there are now jobs in the Jobs folder inside of SQL Server Agent. These aren't very descriptive, are they? Which is which? Let's fix this right now. Double-click Subplan_1 and update your information to match generally what is shown in Figure 4-23. You are going to want to have something in the Name field which generally matches the task at hand, so try not to put something random in that field. Instead, give it a descriptive name. Notice that I have named mine "backrecTestDB.Full Backup."

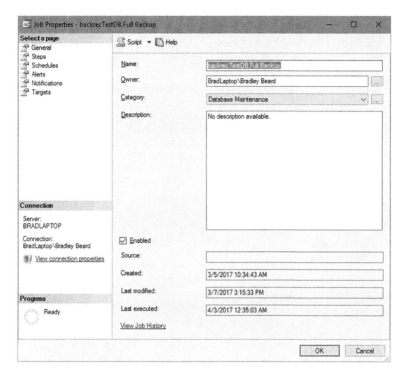

Figure 4-23. *Job Properties, General tab*

Notice that the job is set to Database Maintenance in the Category option. This is great, because this is what we are doing. Ensure that the Enabled check box is checked, and this screen is all set.

One thing I skipped over is the Owner selection. This typically should be set to the owner of the database, although we are specifically referring to the owner of the *task*, and not the owner of the *database*. For that reason, it should be set to any user with heightened permissions in the database.

Also notice that on the left, there are menu options. You are currently on the General option. If you click the Steps option, you will see what is shown in Figure 4-24.

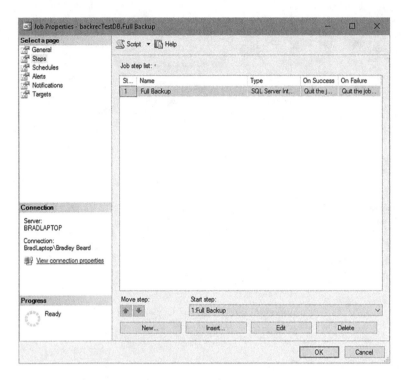

Figure 4-24. *Job Properties, Steps tab*

If you're setting this up for the first time, you will notice that the menu bar does not show your new name yet. Mine is updating because I'm showing the result of the operation. To update your plan name, double-click the text Subplan_1 (as opposed to what I show as full backup in Figure 4-24). The Job Step Properties window opens, so change the Step name box to "Full Backup," as shown in Figure 4-25.

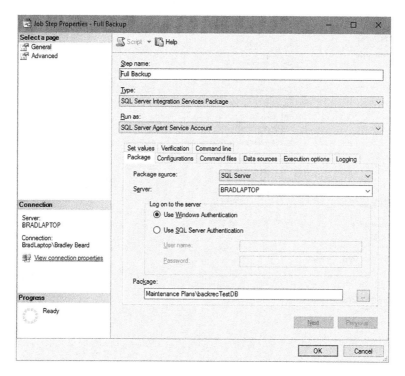

Figure 4-25. *Job Properties, Steps tab, General option*

Don't touch anything else on this screen just yet, except for clicking the Advanced option on the left. Adjust this screen to the settings shown in Figure 4-26.

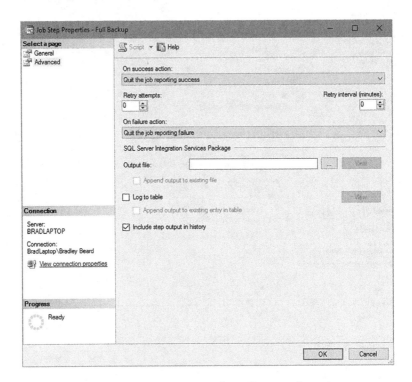

Figure 4-26. *Job Properties, Steps tab, Advanced option*

All I did here was click the *Include step output in history* check box. If you have a table set up to log maintenance plan results to a table in your database, then you could select the *Log to table* check box. Additionally, you could also output the results of the operation to a file by entering in a file location to the *Output file* box.

Click OK when this is done, and you will go back to the Job Properties screen, with the text "Full Backup" now replacing Subplan_1. Figure 4-27 is what you should see now.

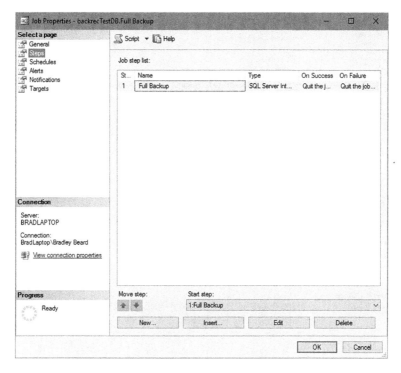

Figure 4-27. *Job Properties, Steps tab*

Click the Schedules option on the left and notice that our schedule is in there, and that it is enabled, as shown in Figure 4-28.

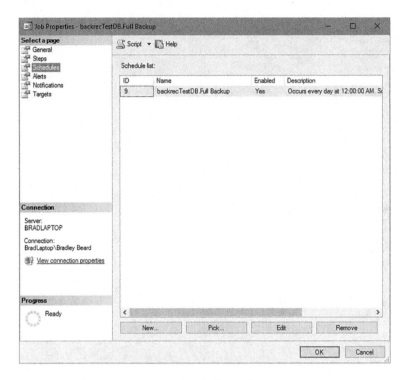

Figure 4-28. *Job Properties, Schedules tab*

Click the Alerts option, and you will see a blank screen. This is fine, for now.

Click the Notifications option, and you will see what is shown in Figure 4-29.

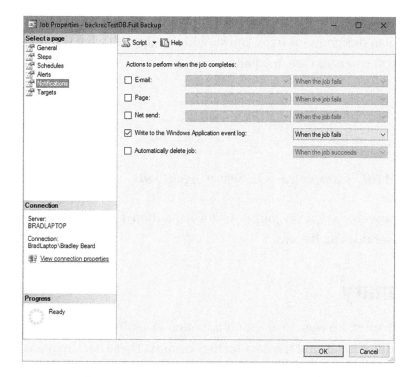

Figure 4-29. *Job Properties, Notifications tab*

If you have an Operator set up and have previously configured Database Mail already, select the Operator in the E-mail box. For the time being, we are going to keep the *Write to the Windows Application event log* option selected, but we are going to change the drop-down to *When the job completes*; that way we will always know what happened with our job.

Clicking the Targets option will show a blank screen as well. This is fine, since we haven't defined any targets.

Click OK when you are through with the Targets option, and have followed the directions for this area.

If you look in the Jobs folder of SQL Server Agent, you will see that this job is renamed and saved as full backup. Do the same things listed previously for the other two and label them accordingly. Remember that we defined the full backup as the first task, differential backup as the second task, and the transaction log as the third task. Those line up with the subplan designations here. You should end up with what is shown in Figure 4-30 when you are finished.

Figure 4-30. *Completed SQL Server Agent jobs*

It's okay that syspolicy_purge_history is in there too. That's a job that SQL Server does on its own.

Summary

In this chapter, we went over the culmination of setting up a backup plan for full, differential, and transaction log backups. These backup plans are entirely dependent upon the recovery model of the database in question, and must be set to either full or bulk-logged models, since simple does not allow for transaction log backups.

We learned the importance of running backups that have verified integrity, and the possible risk we run when not having the backup integrity verified each time it is created.

We clearly and properly defined our backup schedule, based on the needs of a particular environment, and translated those needs into a quantifiable time schedule that creates backups as expected.

Finally, we learned how to make the final backup maintenance plan more easily readable to humans, while maintaining the complexity of the tasks.

We are going to continue into Chapter 5 with the restore equivalent to the backup scenario that we created in Chapter 1. This is the logical extension of the backup scenario, since there is no point in having a backup if you have no means of restoring that backup.

PART II

Restores

CHAPTER 5

Full Restores

Following the format of the previous chapters, we are going to continue on in the journey of backups and restores by delving into the second section of this book. The first section, comprised of Chapters 1–4, covered the backup portion; this second section, comprised of Chapters 5–8, is going to cover the restore portion.

At this point, we realize that a database backup is fundamental to the entire data recovery process. Without a backup, there can be no restore. For that reason, it is vital that the backups taken are correct, which we covered earlier. Now, going further with that rudimentary knowledge, we are going to look at various ways to do a restore of a full database backup.

It is important to point out that database restores are mostly done within SQL Server Management Studio. I would like to stress the term "mostly" here, because it is not the only way to restore data. For example, if your master database has become corrupted, then it must be restored from a full backup before SQL Server will start correctly. This is because master holds all of the configuration information for SQL Server. A major problem with a corrupt master database, beyond the obvious issue of SQL Server not starting, is that all the other system databases (msdb and model) depend on master to function correctly. If master is corrupted badly enough, then the system tables will need to be rebuilt individually, and that is a major headache.

© Bradley Beard 2018
B. Beard, *Beginning Backup and Restore for SQL Server,*
https://doi.org/10.1007/978-1-4842-3456-3_5

What Is a Full Restore?

Simply put, a full restore is exactly what it sounds like, and yet not what it sounds like at all; it restores all of the data contained in a previously run full database backup, but it does not restore the entire database. Recall that the full database backup only backs up the data, and not the system settings. Only the table data for the specified database will be contained in the database backup.

Note   If you need a backup of the system settings as related to the installation of SQL Server, you must have a current backup of the master, msdb, and model databases. These are system databases and are extremely important to the smooth operation of SQL Server.

When I first started working in SQL Server, it was between SQL Server 7 and SQL Server 2000. I was sort of used to how MySQL worked as far as interface and usability, so the switch was a little hard at first, but I gradually got the hang of it. One of the things about MySQL that I really liked was that their "backups" were just huge .sql files with a ton of INSERT commands. That's right, the entirety of the database was dumped in sequence; first, the DROP and CREATE commands for a table, then the individual INSERT statements for all the data in that table. This may seem like a waste of space to some, but the brilliance is in the detail, if you ask me. A DBA with enough time on their hands could then pick through that backup and literally control the insertion of data at a granular level not seen in SQL Server. What I mean by that is that SQL Server does not make backups in this format; backups in SQL Server are made specifically for the SQL Server engine to execute, not for human readability. Yes, in a SQL Server backup, the data is there (obviously), but it can't be read by opening it in Notepad, for example.

Another aspect of full restores is that they can be used to create perfect copies of existing databases. Being able to have this sort of functionality available to me in a development environment is absolutely invaluable, because I can easily create an entire development database based on a production database that I use primarily for testing. I can then create another database, an exact duplicate of the development database, but name it something different. Then, if I ever need to restore the data, I can easily TRUNCATE any table in the first development database and replace the data quickly with an INSERT INTO statement using the second development database as the source and the first development database as the destination. I will show exactly how this is done later in this chapter.

First, let's switch our focus momentarily to the system databases. There are three main system databases, named master, msdb, and model. These three databases carry the configuration information for your SQL Server installation, so they are extremely important to the overall health of your entire installation. Technically, there is a fourth system database named tempdb, but this database is destroyed and created every time an instance of SQL Server is created for that particular instance of SQL Server, so it's not necessary to worry about backing it up.

Restoring the Master Database

If you ever have to restore the master database, or any of the system databases, I sincerely hope it is not because of a major corruption issue. I can tell you first-hand that this is a major undertaking, and must be done with the utmost care and attention to detail. This section will show the individual steps and instructions for restoring the master database from a full database backup. The steps can be applied to restore any system database, but for now, I will only focus on the master database.

This section is dependent on the presence of a current backup of the master database. It is usually best to make a backup of the master database every time that a change is made to the structure of the tables or to the underlying architecture of the database. Backing up the master database and having it available in case of emergency will alleviate a lot of problems in the future, and I would recommend backing up these system databases as part of your normal backup maintenance plan. I didn't cover this in the previous chapters dealing with backups because the content for this book is based on your individual database backups, and not the next level of database administration, where we would be dealing with the backups of the system databases as well. To continue, run a quick backup of the master database, or use one that you have already prepared.

The first thing that we have to do to restore the master database is start SQL Server in single-user mode. For those that are new to this operation, single-user mode starts SQL Server with a limited number of connections (one) so that emergency work can be done without additional burden to the server.

Start SQL Server in Single-User Mode

Step-by-step instructions to put SQL Server into single-user mode are as follows.

- Open up SQL Server Configuration Manager or, if you're on Windows 10, open the Start menu and type *sqlservermanager13.msc,* press Enter, and look for the SQL Server (MSSQLSERVER) item in the right pane.

- Right-click and select Properties, then select the Startup Parameters tab.

- Type −m in the Specify a startup parameter field.

- Click the Add button.

- Click Apply and notice that a message appears that tells us that our changes will not take effect until you restart the service. We will restart the service momentarily. Click OK on this message, and then click OK on the SQL Server (MSSQLSERVER) Properties window to close it.

- Click the SQL Server Agent item and press the Stop Service button in the toolbar.

- Restart the SQL Server (MSSQLSERVER) service.

These directions set our instance of SQL Server to single-user mode. Let's get into the details of these directions a lot deeper though, so we really know what we're working toward.

To get SQL Server started in single-user mode, we have to open up our SQL Server Configuration Manager. This is somewhat hard to find, but if you're on SQL Server 2016 and Windows 10, just open the Start menu and type *sqlservermanager13.msc* and press Enter. Figure 5-1 shows the screen you should see at this point.

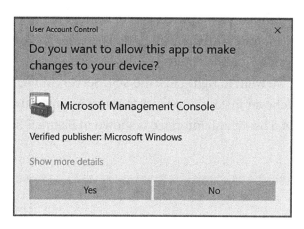

***Figure 5-1.** User Account Control*

We want to click Yes here in order to proceed. The next screen that opens is the SQL Server Configuration Manager, as shown in Figure 5-2.

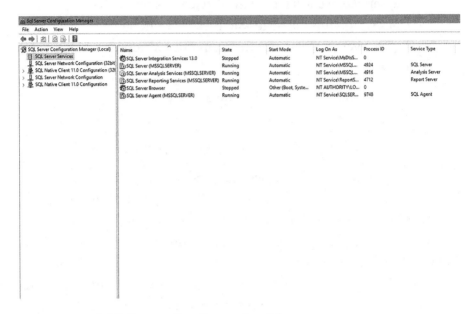

Figure 5-2. *SQL Server Configuration Manager*

If you aren't familiar with the SQL Server Configuration Manager interface, I would spend a little time in here. There are an awful lot of configuration options in this section.

To proceed, we want to right-click the SQL Server (MSSQLSERVER) instance, or whichever instance you want to start in single-user mode, and select Properties. The default interface is shown in Figure 5-3.

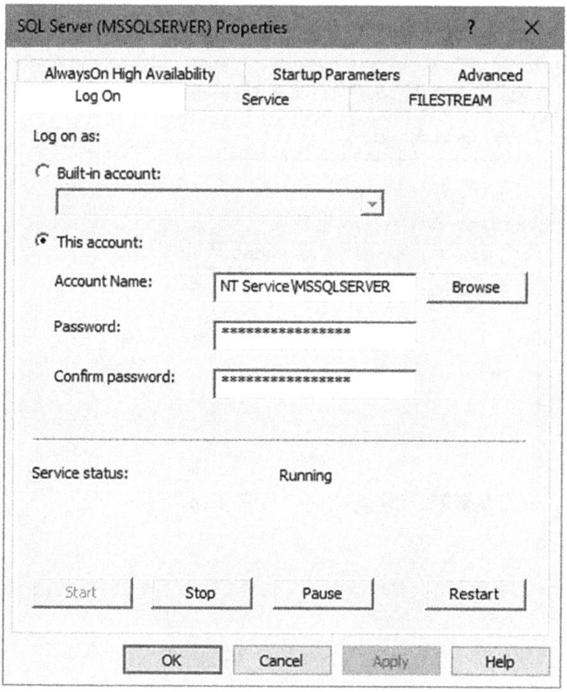

Figure 5-3. *SQL Server (MSSQLSERVER) Properties, Log On tab*

Note that the default tab selected is named Log On. We want to click the Startup Parameters tab at the top of the screen to open the screen shown in Figure 5-4.

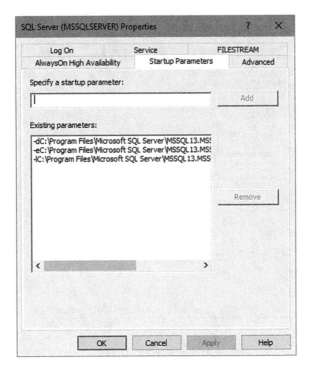

Figure 5-4. *SQL Server (MSSQLSERVER) Properties, Startup Parameters tab*

The text box labeled Specify a startup parameter is where we are going to enter the text –m. That is the startup parameter needed to start SQL Server in single-user mode. Enter that value and click the Add button, which will become enabled once a parameter has been entered into the parameter field. Figure 5-5 shows what you should see after entering –m in the startup parameter field.

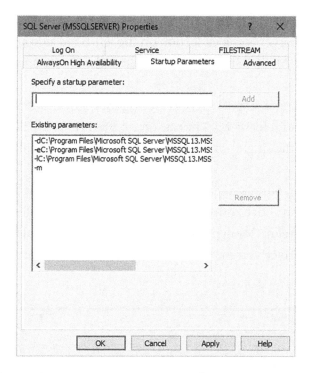

Figure 5-5. *-m startup parameter entered*

At this point, we want to click Apply to save the changes, and we are immediately presented with the dialog box shown in Figure 5-6.

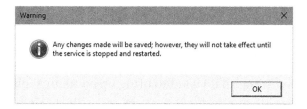

Figure 5-6. *Warning*

That message is telling us that we need to bounce the SQL Server service, so click OK here, and then click OK on the SQL Server (MSSQLSERVER) Properties window. That should bring us back to the SQL Server Configuration Manager interface we saw in Figure 5-2.

In the SQL Server Configuration Manager interface, make sure that you are in the SQL Server Services section on the left-hand side and right-click the SQL Server (MSSQLSERVER) item in the right-hand panel and select Restart.

Next, we want to stop the SQL Server Agent service, so right-click SQL Server Agent and select Stop. The reason for this is because SQL Server Agent will take the single connection that is available to the database if it is running.

At this point, our instance of SQL Server is running in single-user mode without an active connection. Start SSMS and you will see your regular login screen. Connect as normal here, and you should proceed to the regular interface you see once starting SSMS. My interface is shown in Figure 5-7.

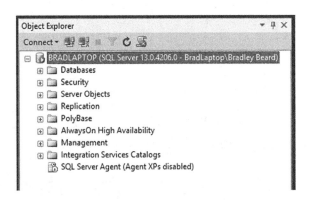

Figure 5-7. My SSMS interface

There are two things that I want to bring up about this initial screen: first, there isn't an obvious indication that I am in single-user mode, and second, the SQL Server Agent is shown as disabled. So how do we know that we are in single-user mode? Simple. We know that single-user mode means that only a single user can log in to the database engine at a time, right? So what do you think would happen if we were to log in again using the same account we are already logged in with?

Click the Connect drop-down in the Object Explorer pane. Choose
Database Engine... and you will see the normal login screen. Log in
normally, and what do you see? Figure 5-8 details my response from SQL
Server.

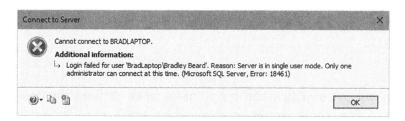

Figure 5-8. *Connect to Server*

Right there in black and light gray is the explanation that we are
currently in single-user mode. Click OK and then click Cancel to get back
to the regular SSMS screen. Open up a New Query window and notice
that you are connected to the master database. We could begin to work
normally here, with the obvious exception that SQL Server Agent will
not be running, so we can't do anything that requires SQL Server Agent.
A simple script to create a backup of the system databases is shown in
Listing 5-1.

Listing 5-1. Backup Script for System Databases

```
USE master
GO
-- Back up the model database
BACKUP DATABASE Model
TO DISK = 'E:\SQL Server\Backup\Model.BAK'
WITH INIT
GO
-- Back up the master database
BACKUP DATABASE Master
```

```
TO DISK = 'E:\SQL Server\Backup\Master.BAK'
WITH INIT
GO
-- Back up the msdb database
BACKUP DATABASE MSDB
TO DISK = 'E:\SQL Server\Backup\MSDB.BAK'
WITH INIT
GO
```

That will give us a good starting point for restoring those databases. The script to restore the system databases is shown in Listing 5-2.

Listing 5-2. Restore Script for System Databases

```
RESTORE DATABASE master FROM DISK = 'E:\SQL Server\Backup\
Master.BAK' WITH REPLACE;
RESTORE DATABASE model FROM DISK = 'E:\SQL Server\Backup\Model.
BAK' WITH REPLACE;
RESTORE DATABASE msdb FROM DISK = 'E:\SQL Server\Backup\MSDB.
BAK' WITH REPLACE;
```

Microsoft generally recommends that the sqlcmd utility is used for restoring system databases, so let's open a command prompt, type sqlcmd, and press Enter. Figure 5-9 shows what happened what I tried to start sqlcmd.

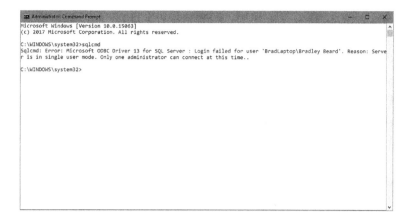

Figure 5-9. *Trying to start sqlcmd*

There's our "error" again. It's not really an error, but more of an
annoying reminder that we are in single-user mode. Not a problem
though; we just need to close SSMS and rerun the sqlcmd command. It
should work for you now; if it doesn't, restart the SQL Server service and
rerun the command. We will then see what is shown in Figure 5-10.

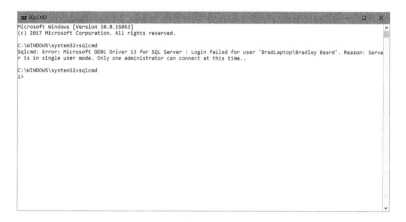

Figure 5-10. *sqlcmd*

We can see that the `sqlcmd` utility has started because we now have the first line under the `sqlcmd` command showing a prompt of 1>. This means that `sqlcmd` is awaiting a command. At this prompt, type RESTORE DATABASE master FROM DISK = 'E:\SQL Server\Backup\Master.BAK' WITH REPLACE; and press Enter. You will then have a prompt of 2>. All you need to type here is GO and press Enter. Your screen should closely resemble what is shown in Figure 5-11.

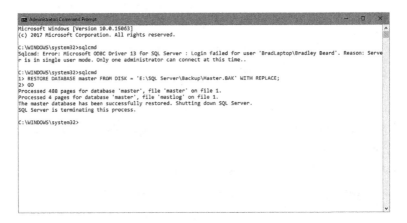

Figure 5-11. *Operation complete*

That shows us that the master database was successfully restored, and that the process was terminated normally. Before we are done, we need to bounce the SQL Server service, so open up Services and restart the SQL Server (MSSQLSERVER) service (or whichever named instance you are working in). You will not be able to reconnect to the database instance until the server is rebooted or the service is bounced.

Restore SQL Server to Multiuser Mode

In my opinion, restoring access to SQL Server is easier than restricting access. Step-by-step instructions to restore SQL Server back to its original state (i.e., multiuser mode) are as follows:

- Open up *sqlservermanager13.msc* again and look for the SQL Server (MSSQLSERVER) item in the right pane.

- Right-click and select Properties, then select the Startup Parameters tab.

- Highlight the –m entry and click the Remove button.

- Click Apply and notice that a message appears that prompts us to restart the SQL Server service. Click OK on this message, and then click OK on the SQL Server (MSSQLSERVER) Properties window to close it.

- Click the SQL Server Agent item and press the Start Service button in the toolbar.

- Click the SQL Server (MSSQLSERVER) item again and press the Restart Service button in the toolbar.

These directions set our instance of SQL Server back to multiuser mode. Congratulations! You have just set SQL Server to single-user mode, restored the master database, and restored SQL Server to multiuser mode.

Restoring from a Full Backup

By now in this chapter, you've probably gotten a pretty good idea of how to restore a database from a full backup. Every single DBA that I know has had to run a restore at one point or another, so this shouldn't be anything new. In case this is new territory, this section will cover not only how to restore from a full backup using SSMS and T-SQL, but also some of the finer points of restoring data, such as restoring to a specific point within a log backup (called a point-in-time restore).

Full Restores with SSMS

The most common way to restore a database is by using the graphical interface that is most commonly associated with SQL Server. SQL Server Management Studio offers a vast array of tools that can be used to manipulate and administer a database, and for this reason, it is easily the go-to choice for nearly every SQL Server administrator. Notice that I say "nearly" here; that's because there are obvious exceptions to every rule, and this is not an insult or derision in any way. I have seen SQL Server administrators using legacy SSDT, for example, because they got (most) of the same interaction with the database, with the added value of having the interface for Visual Studio available to them for writing DTSX packages or whatever else they would have needed the enhanced interface to accomplish.

The first thing we want to do is locate our latest backup set. If you have your directories set up like mine, then they are in E:\SQL Server\Backup.

Next, fire up SSMS and expand Databases. Inside of the Databases menu, you will find your user databases, along with ReportServer and ReportServerTempDB, if you have installed SQL Server reporting services. Find the database you want to work with (in this case, backrecTestDB), right-click it, hover over Tasks, then hover over Restore, and look at the options available to us. Figure 5-12 shows the interface at this point.

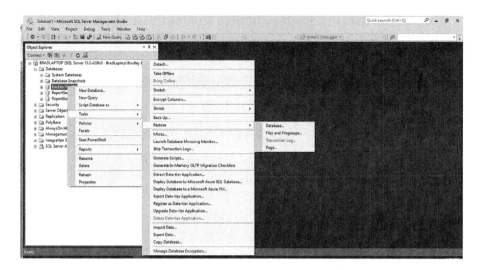

Figure 5-12. *SSMS Restore menu*

Inside the Restore menu, we can see four options listed. Those options are

- Database

- Files and filegroups

- Transaction log

- Page

First off, why is the transaction log option disabled? It can only be enabled when the database was restored using a full backup and RESTORE WITH STANDBY was enabled at the point of restore. The database would then be standing by (in RecoveryPending mode), waiting for the restoration of the tail of the transaction log. If you were to recover a database using RESTORE WITH STANDBY, and then want to restore the transaction log, the transaction log option would be the only available option, and the other three options would be disabled.

We want to select the database option, so click this and you will see something similar to what is shown in Figure 5-13.

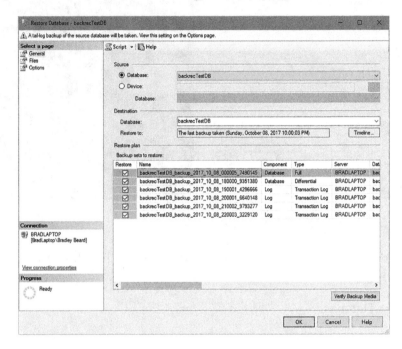

Figure 5-13. *Restore Database window, General tab*

Notice that the *Backup sets to restore:* section already has the latest backup sets enabled and ready to be restored. From top to bottom, we can see that there is one full, one differential, and four transaction log backups that we can use to restore our database. Also note that there are check boxes to the left so we can choose which set of data to restore. You can see how deselecting the differential option will not deselect the transaction log options, and selecting a transaction log option automatically selects the differential option.

The exact combination of files you will need to restore to the point you are looking for is entirely up to you. You can use as many or as few backup sets as you would like.

For this example, referring to Figure 5-13, we can see that there are only a few files selected for the restore to the last transaction log backup. To restore to this point, we need to restore the latest full and differential backups, then the transaction logs, in order. Let's say that we want to restore back to the previous day though. The way that I have my backups set up is such that I will only ever need to restore up to seven files. The reason for this is explained in Table 5-1, which is referenced from Chapter 4.

Table 5-1. *My 24-Hour Backup Schedule*

Time	Full?	Differential?	Transaction Log?
12:00 AM	X	X	X
1:00 AM			X
2:00 AM			X
3:00 AM			X
4:00 AM			X
5:00 AM			X
6:00 AM		X	X
7:00 AM			X
8:00 AM			X
9:00 AM			X
10:00 AM			X
11:00 AM			X
12:00 PM		X	X
1:00 PM			X
2:00 PM			X

(*continued*)

111

Table 5-1. (*continued*)

Time	Full?	Differential?	Transaction Log?
3:00 PM			X
4:00 PM			X
5:00 PM			X
6:00 PM		X	X
7:00 PM			X
8:00 PM			X
9:00 PM			X
10:00 PM			X
11:00 PM			X

You can see from this schedule that, as I said earlier, I will only ever need to restore a maximum of seven files; one full backup, one differential backup, and five transaction log backups. This schedule also implies that I will only lose, at a maximum, one hour's worth of data. That will only be the case when data loss occurs immediately after a transaction log is run, so the transactions for the next hour are deemed suspect, because the transaction log may not restore correctly.

Going back to what we see in Figure 5-13, that tells me that I am restoring from the latest database backup available. This is probably the most common restore, since we want to recover to a certain point in the recent past. This isn't always the case though, and we can specify whether we want to use the default, latest backups presented to us from within the Source section of Figure 5-13 or whether we want to choose a set of backups from the past that are not shown in the *Backup sets to restore:* section at the bottom of Figure 5-13. The top section, labeled Source, has two options:

- Database: Allows you to restore to the latest backup set consisting of full, differential, and any applicable transaction log backups, depending on the time the restore is started.

- Device: Allows you to pick any backup set from the file system to restore from. SQL Server will let you know if the backup set selected in this section is unable to be restored for some reason.

The database option is selected in the Source section. Beneath the Source is the Destination section. This section lets you pick the database to restore to, and a point in time to restore to as well. We will get into point-in-time restores more deeply in the next section. The applicable full, differential, and transaction log backups are shown in the Restore plan section of the interface. On the left side of the Restore Database window, we can see that there are three menu options: General, Files, and Options. For now, let's leave the General tab alone and click the Files menu section on the left. Figure 5-14 shows the Files section.

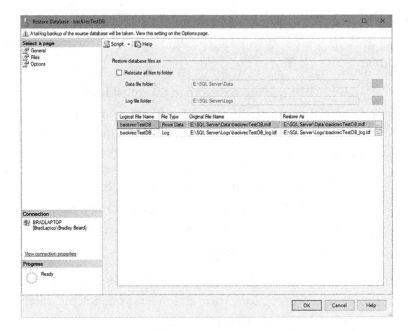

Figure 5-14. *Restore Database window, Files tab*

This information comes from the default settings for your installation. Notice that my default file locations are already selected for me. As you can see, the restore process is going to write new files to the locations specified, unless new locations are entered in the Restore As field (the rightmost field in the lower part of the interface). Select the Options menu item on the left to move to the next section. Figure 5-15 shows what this default interface looks like.

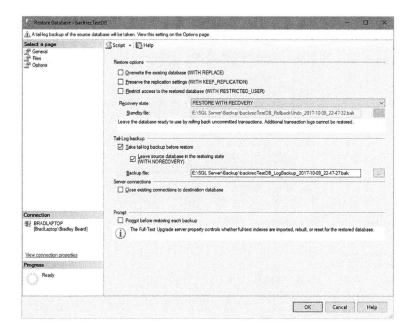

Figure 5-15. *Restore Database window, Options tab*

For a general restore, I usually select the Overwrite the existing database (WITH REPLACE) and deselect the Leave source database in the restoring state (WITH NORECOVERY) option and leave the rest as default. This lets me overwrite everything in the database up to the point of failure, and does not keep my database locked and unable to be recovered, just in case of another catastrophic event. When you have chosen the options that you need for your scenario, press the OK button. Figure 5-16 shows what you should see after clicking OK.

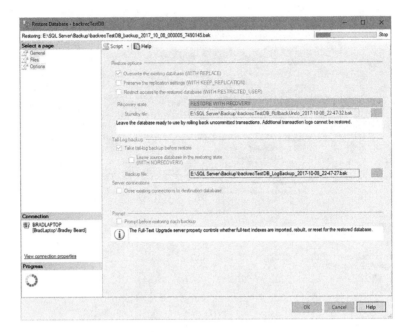

Figure 5-16. *Restore Database, Restoring action*

This will take a little while to run, depending on the size of your backups. Mine took about 20 seconds to complete, since I didn't have a huge amount of data to restore. Eventually, you should see what is shown in Figure 5-17.

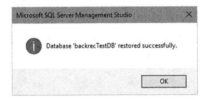

Figure 5-17. *Restore successful*

Success! This message obviously means that our database was restored successfully. To check that this operation was successful (employ the adage of "Trust, but Verify"), simply run the code in Listing 5-3.

Listing 5-3. Trust, but Verify

```
SELECT RH.[destination_database_name] as 'Database',
RH.[restore_date] as 'Restore Date',
BS.[backup_start_date] as 'Backup Start Date',
BS.[backup_finish_date] as 'Backup Finish Date',
BS.[database_name] as 'Source Database',
BMF.[physical_device_name] as 'Backup Filename'
FROM [msdb].[dbo].[restorehistory] RH
INNER JOIN [msdb].[dbo].[backupset] BS
ON RH.[backup_set_id] = BS.[backup_set_id]
INNER JOIN [msdb].[dbo].[backupmediafamily] BMF
ON BS.[media_set_id] = BMF.[media_set_id]
WHERE( MONTH([restore_date]) = MONTH(getDate())
AND DAY([restore_date]) = DAY(getDate())
AND YEAR([restore_date]) = YEAR(getDate()))
ORDER BY RH.[restore_date]
```

Running this code will show us what is shown in Figure 5-18. Note that your results may vary, depending on the restore dates, file names, and database name.

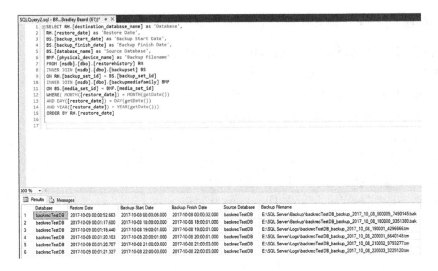

Figure 5-18. Trust, but Verify results

There is proof that our backup was complete, and the restore was successful. Also note that there are the same six files listed, in order, that we previously saw in the General tab in Figure 5-1. Go ahead and flip back to that figure and check the file name in Figure 5-13 against the file name in Figure 5-18. They are identical, which again proves that our operation was a success.

Restoring to a Point in Time

You can consider yourself extremely fortunate if you have not had a catastrophic failure in your database. I can count on one hand the number of times that I have had to spend a day searching for log files and applying backups, and sometimes, those backups were either outdated or corrupt. "Frustrating" doesn't really begin to describe how I felt at those times; I think "enraged" is probably a more apt description.

More than likely, there will come a time when you will need to restore to a particular point in time, and you are going to need to act quickly to restore the necessary data. In situations like this, there are a few different ways that you can approach the situation: one way is to follow these directions for a point-in-time restore, and another is to fully restore the database to another database instance and restore the data you need from the restored tables in the secondary database. I describe this at length in the section titled "Emergency Full Restore Example" in this chapter. For now, we will focus on point-in-time restores.

Let's start by really messing up our database, shall we? Let's drop our users1 table. That should let us generate a fairly sizeable transaction in the tail of our transaction log to recover from. Our starting record count is 20030001 rows, just for comparison purposes after the restore operation is complete. Simply type DROP TABLE users1; in a New Query window and press F5 or the Execute button in the toolbar to execute the query. Next, execute the statement SELECT count(*) as cnt FROM users1; and you will get the message Invalid object name 'users1'. We can also refresh our Tables in Object Explorer and verify that users1 is definitely gone now.

To continue, right-click your database (backrecTestDB, in my case), expand Tasks, and then expand Restore, and you should see what is shown in Figure 5-19.

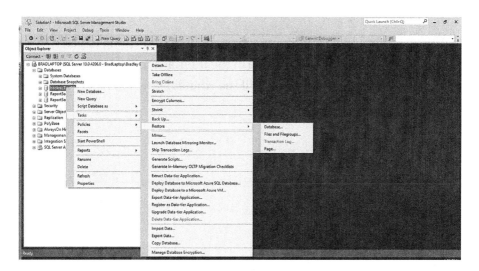

Figure 5-19. *Location of Restore menu items*

Click Database, and you will be shown an interface similar to Figure 5-20. This is also similar to what we saw earlier in Figure 5-13.

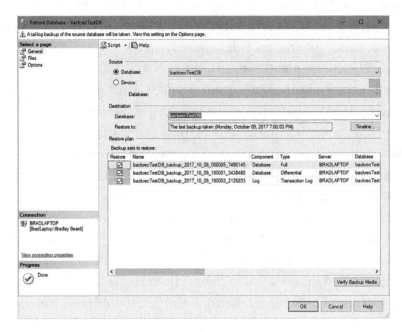

Figure 5-20. *Restore Database screen*

This page should be familiar to you by now. We are going to press the Timeline button on the right side of the interface to continue. After pressing the Timeline button, you will see what is shown in Figure 5-21.

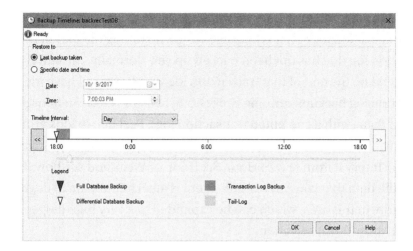

Figure 5-21. *Backup Timeline, Last backup taken*

The default option is Last backup taken. This is exactly the same as just pressing OK on the previous screen; it restores based on what files are available to be restored, and that's all.

We want to click the Specific date and time radio button in order to see what we can restore. Notice how the interface changes to what is shown in Figure 5-22.

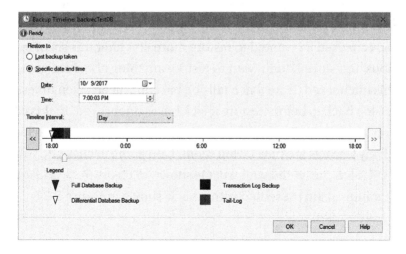

Figure 5-22. *Backup Timeline, Specific date and time*

121

See how the Timeline Interval value has changed to include the tail of the transaction log? That is because we are including the part of the transaction log that has not been backed up yet. Normally, the cutoff time would be the end of that transaction log, and because I have my transaction log backups running every hour, I can only lose an hour's worth of data (with a corrupted transaction log). Feel free to look around in here without pressing the OK button. For example, you can change the Timeline Interval from Day to Hour, Six Hour, or Week and see how that affects the data that you can restore. There is an extremely small degree of granularity in this area, which can be expanded to a very high degree with a simple drop-down selection.

Once you are ready to continue on, move the slider bar under the Timeline Interval to the desired point in time you wish to restore to, and press OK. For this example, I am going to restore to 6:40:31 PM on 10/9/2017, since I know that was before I dropped my users1 table. I do not need to do anything else on the General tab, and the Files tab is okay as well. Skip over to the Options tab, where we want to check the Overwrite the existing database (WITH REPLACE) option and uncheck the Leave source database in the restoring state (WITH NORECOVERY) check box before pressing OK to begin the restore process. I would want to leave the Leave source database in the restoring state (WITH NORECOVERY) check box checked if I wanted to restore more files after this set of restore operations, but since I don't want to restore anything else, I am going to leave this unchecked. Note that a tail-log backup will be taken unless the Take tail-log backup before restore check box is unchecked. In this case, I am going to leave the Take tail-log backup before restore option selected. Once all my settings are how I want them, I am going to click OK. After I press OK, I am presented with what is shown in Figure 5-23, and after about a minute, I am presented with what is shown in Figure 5-24.

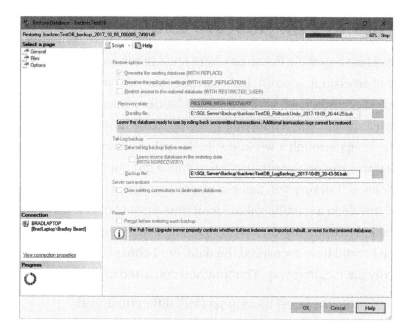

Figure 5-23. *Restore Database*

Figure 5-24. *Restore successful*

At this point, I know that my database has restored successfully.
However, I still want to verify that SQL Server actually did what it was
supposed to do (remember, Trust but Verify). Let's run the simple script we
ran before, `SELECT count(*) as cnt FROM users1;`, and view the results.
The query runs for a few seconds, and then returns the value 20030001.
Exactly as we had initially! Therefore, we can safely assume that this
database has been completely restored as of the time that we selected in
the Timeline area.

Emergency Full Restore Example

Recently, I had a specific instance where I had to restore production data because of an error in a script. Let's assume that you have a table with hundreds of records, each with a unique identifier. Each of these records dealt with a specific set of data that was vital to the normal operation of particular items through a workflow. Let's further assume that the update script that was run on the production instance did not have a WHERE clause defined. I'm sure you can see where everything went sideways... I updated a table to a specific value for all rows instead of just the one row that I needed to update. Now, in this instance, there are lot of different ways that I could have recovered the data, but I chose the quickest and not necessarily the cleanest way. That method consisted of the following steps:

- Locate the latest backup set (full, differential, and transaction log)

- Restore the latest full backup to a new database called fixYourMistake

- Restore the latest differential backup to the fixYourMistake database

- Restore the transaction log backups since the differential back to the fixYourMistake database

- Create an alternate table in the production database called (tablename)_archive, where (tablename) is the name of my table

- Write an INSERT INTO...SELECT statement to write the contents of the original (tablename) into the archive table

- Write a TRUNCATE statement to clear the original table

- Write an INSERT INTO…SELECT statement to insert the restored data from the fixYourMistake database into the production database

You may be asking yourself why I didn't just restore the latest transaction log to the production database to complete the operation quicker. I didn't do this because I wasn't sure if there was going to be any other residual damage to the database, so I wanted to have a solid backup to restore from, just in case. I also did not want to restore the entire database since there were critical operations being entered as this was going on. After I restored the table in question and verified that the data recovery was correct with no other corruption, I had a small amount of cleanup to do on the database server. To clean up after this recovery, I just had to DROP the fixYourMistake database and DROP the archive table that I created earlier. After that, the database was humming along happily, and believe it or not, no one except me was even aware that there was a problem with the database.

I would like to point out that this would not have been possible without a solid backup and restore structure in place. I could not have restored to the last transaction log without a previous backup to recover the data to, and that means that I would have lost data—in a production environment—since the last full backup. That is very, very bad news and I think it goes without saying that scripts being executed on the production environment have been much more highly scrutinized since then. So, I guess you could say that, when this was going on, I was both my own worst enemy and my own best friend at the same time. In the future, I think fewer enemies would be a good thing.

Summary

In this chapter, we learned about the essence of restoring a full backup to a database. We reviewed the importance of having the full recovery model in our databases so that we have access to the full range of backup and restore functionality available within SQL Server.

We looked at point-in-time restores, and covered the basics of the various interfaces in the Restore section of SSMS. There is a wealth of information in these various sections, and I encourage you to create a spare database in SSMS, restore to this new database, and play with the settings until you are comfortable with what the various settings and options are really doing behind the scenes.

The principles we have picked up here can be mostly transferred to the differential and transaction log restore areas, with slight changes due to the nature of the backups themselves. For example, the process to select a differential backup is similar as far as the interface is concerned, but the functionality and purpose are completely different from the other two restore types.

CHAPTER 6

Differential Restores

Back in Chapter 2, we went over the fundamentals of differential backups and how important the differential base is to the overall recovery strategy. Those same principals apply to differential restores, except that we are now dealing with the other end of the transaction, so to speak. The choice of recovery models is the single most important aspect to determining the efficacy of the restore methods that are available to you. Recall that we used the full recovery model for our test database; this means that we have access to the full range of backup and restore functionality for our database. Had we chosen the bulk-logged recovery model, we would have gotten most of the same functionality, but if we had bulk-logged transactions in the transaction log, we would have sacrificed the capability to restore to a point in time as we did in Chapter 5. A bulk-logged recovery model would allow us to recover only to the end of a backup; in other words, every backup must be fully recovered, or no data restore will take place at all.

Restoring data in SQL Server from a differential backup is almost the same as restoring data from a full backup, with a few obvious differences. First, the most obvious point to make is that a differential backup can only be restored to the corresponding full backup. This is because the differential backup is the last set of data taken from the backed-up transaction logs and changed data since the last full backup, referred to as the "base" back in Chapter 2. So, if you try to restore a differential backup out of sequence, it will fail. The sequence of data will not line up, and SQL Server will halt the restore operation. Second, the database must be

© Bradley Beard 2018
B. Beard, *Beginning Backup and Restore for SQL Server*,
https://doi.org/10.1007/978-1-4842-3456-3_6

in the NORECOVERY or STANDBY mode to restore a differential backup. The reason for this is because the database can only restore a differential backup to a full backup; it cannot restore just a differential backup without first restoring the full backup. Once the full backup is restored, then the database can be placed into NORECOVERY or STANDBY mode.

Let's briefly go over the recovery state options that are available when restoring a database. These options control the state of the database after the restore has completed and can change with each restore type.

- RESTORE WITH RECOVERY: This is the default and means that the database is ready for use immediately after the recovery process is complete. The implication is that the entire database restore operation is complete, meaning that additional transaction logs cannot be restored.

- RESTORE WITH NORECOVERY: This option does not leave the database in a ready state, which means it is not operational after the restore operation is complete. With this option, transaction logs can continue to be restored normally. The database cannot be put into the ready state until a final command using the WITH RECOVERY option is executed against the database.

- RESTORE WITH STANDBY: Finally, this option leaves the database in the standby mode, which is essentially read-only. Any transaction that has not been committed to the transaction log is undone, and the undo actions are saved in a standby file.

Remember in Chapter 5 how we checked the Leave source database in the restoring state (WITH NORECOVERY) option checked? That allowed us to still have the option to restore more backups, specifically the differential and any subsequent transaction log backups, which we will get to in Chapter 7.

What Is a Differential Restore?

Simply put, a differential restore is the restoration of data from a differential backup. We know that a differential backup is only the changed data since the last full backup, so it is a smaller file than a full backup.

So how does this fit into our backup strategy? Our full backups run every morning at 12:00 AM, our differential backups run every six hours, and our transaction log backups run every hour. In other words, I personally think it is a pretty solid backup schedule. The usage of the full or simple recovery models, and of implementing differential backups and restores, has a few very distinct implications:

- We can have fewer transaction logs and therefore fewer overall files in our backup plan, since we can delete all transaction logs before the last full backup was taken, assuming that the data from these transaction logs is already resident in the differential backups.

- We have a lot more recovery points, or places that we can restore to, available to us.

- Backups can take place during the day without having to run a full backup every time. This will cut down on server CPU time and require less space.

We can see that using differential backups and restores as part of our normal database recovery plan is the best way to go for what we decided was our ideal recovery scenario.

Restoring Using SSMS

I hope that by now, we all have a little bit of experience doing database restores using SQL Server Management Studio. If you read my first book, I relied heavily on maintenance plan creation to handle the entirety of daily database maintenance. This included a backup method that could eventually be used for restoring data, complete with full, differential, and transaction log backups. We don't want to go quite that far yet, since that is what we will cover in later chapters once we tie everything together, but we do want to look at how differential restores are handled in SQL Server Management Studio.

Go ahead and start SSMS, if you haven't already. You should see the interface with Object Explorer to the left and nothing in the stage. I generally keep a New Query window open in the main stage, but it's not necessary. Once you have SSMS open and are ready to move on, expand Databases, right-click your test database name (mine is backrecTestDB), and hover over Tasks, then Restore, and finally, select Database... to continue. Figure 6-1 shows the location of this menu item.

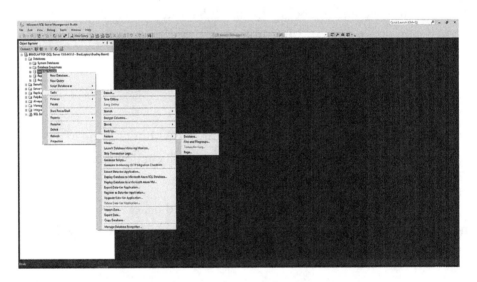

Figure 6-1. *Database menu item location*

After selecting Database as shown in Figure 6-1, you will see the screen shown in Figure 6-2.

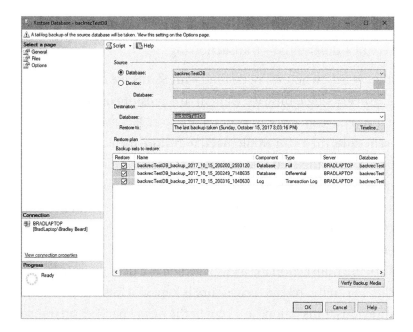

Figure 6-2. *Restore Database*

This is the regular screen that we have seen before each time we want to restore our database. Note that all available backups for this database are available as shown in Figure 6-2, and I have deleted a few backups from the file system to make the interface a bit cleaner.

Verify in your interface that all check boxes next to the three backups listed (or however many you have and want to restore) are checked. Since we want to restore our differential backup, we must restore the full backup first, and we must keep the database in the restoring state in order to continue restoring our differential backups and our transaction logs. If you were to uncheck all the recovery options, you would view the available combinations of restorations that can be done within the database. Those combinations are as follows:

- Full

- Full + differential

131

- Full + transaction log

- Full + differential + transaction log

In other words, when we're dealing with SSMS, we must start with a full backup every single time we want to run a restore operation. Think of it like this: if you have an error in your database at 3:05 PM, under my current backup schedule, then you would need to restore the last full backup from that morning, then the 12:00 PM differential backup, and finally, each hourly transaction log until you recover the data you need.

Notice that we are on the General tab of the Restore Database screen. We have already gone through the various options in these tabs, so we don't need to go through them again. Note that we will be taking a backup of the tail of the transaction log as well, which is a default option so that the transaction to run the restore procedure is kept in a fresh transaction log, and the previous transactions are kept in the newly backed-up transaction log tail.

Since we are restoring the differential backup, we just need to make sure that the full and differential backup options are selected on the General tab, and then press OK. We will then wait for a few seconds, or possibly longer, and see what is shown in Figure 6-3.

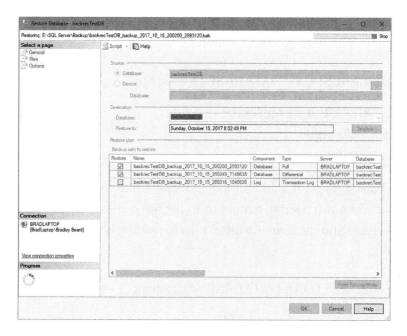

Figure 6-3. *Restore Database in progress*

Hopefully, we will see a success message eventually. Click OK on this message, and the Restore Database screen goes away. This signifies that our database has been restored to the data relevant to the differential backup.

Restoring Using T-SQL

The process for restoring a differential backup using T-SQL is surprisingly easy. Up until this point, I didn't include a whole lot of SQL because I wanted to make these books geared more toward the visual aspect of database administration, but I think that this warrants a bit of time.

The real strength of using T-SQL, apart from automation purposes, is that you can use sqlcmd to execute the SQL statements if you cannot get to the interface for SQL but still have access to the database server.

The basic syntax for a differential restore with a logical backup device and no other files to restore is shown in Listing 6-1.

Listing 6-1. RESTORE DATABASE SQL Script

```
RESTORE DATABASE backrecTestDB
FROM backrecTestDB
WITH NORECOVERY
```

The basic syntax for a differential restore without a defined backup device, or when you need to restore from the file system and not a logical backup device and there are no other files to restore, is shown in Listing 6-2.

Listing 6-2. RESTORE DATABASE SQL Script

```
RESTORE DATABASE backrecTestDB
FROM DISK = 'E:\SQL Server\Backup\backrecTestDB\backrecTestDB_
DIFF.bak'
WITH NORECOVERY
```

Keep in mind that when restoring a differential backup, when we specify NORECOVERY, what we are saying is that we want to restore the last full backup, and then the differential backup. The reason for this is because, as we discussed earlier, we must have a logical starting point for all restores, and the only place to do that is with the last full backup, which is the highest level of restore for the period. From that point, we can then filter down the differential backups, and finally, into the transaction logs to get to the precise location of the data restoration. We also want to specify NORECOVERY if we have additional transaction logs to restore; otherwise, we would specify RECOVERY instead.

If you were to execute the code in Listing 6-1, considering that you had a logical backup device defined and didn't have any other files to restore (i.e., additional transaction logs), you would end up with the same result as executing a differential restore as we did previously. The same result would happen with Listing 6-2, if you needed to restore from the file system and not from a logical backup device.

Summary

This is the shortest chapter in this book, simply because the concept of differential restores is based on the preceding full backup. In other words, if you have the full backup, then you can hopefully start restoring the data that you need whether that data resides in the differential backup or the transaction logs. Restoring the differential backup could be thought of as a logical extension of restoring the full backup, since the existence of the differential restore is predicated on the existence of the full backup already having been restored, but as we noted before, you could always restore from the transaction log instead, if that is the data that you need.

We went over how to restore a differential backup from both SSMS and straight SQL, and briefly went over the different options relevant to this type of restore. Be sure to include the syntax that we went over in Listing 6-1 and Listing 6-2 for your situation in the restore script that you need to write.

In the next chapter, we will go over how to restore transaction logs and the different options that can be enabled or disabled in this area.

CHAPTER 7

Transaction Log Restores

Restoring a transaction log in SQL Server can be surprisingly painless. There are a few things to consider before you attempt to restore your transaction log though, such as the following:

- Do you need to restore to a specific point in time?

- Are you attempting to recover from a catastrophic database failure?

- Do you even have transaction logs to restore?

These questions, and sometimes many more, need to be addressed in order to lead you down the correct path of transaction log restoration. There have been lots of times that I was alerted to an incident within one of my databases, and I didn't stop to consider which route I needed to take: I just took off down the ill-lighted path of "restore something or other." In other words, I knew that I needed to restore *some* data, but I didn't really know specifically *what* data needed to be restored. I didn't know which tables were affected, if any, or if everything after a certain point in time was affected.

For this reason, it is always best to consider the following bit of free advice: take as much time as you need to gather the **correct** information

© Bradley Beard 2018
B. Beard, *Beginning Backup and Restore for SQL Server*,
https://doi.org/10.1007/978-1-4842-3456-3_7

and formulate a workable plan before attempting to restore your transaction logs. You can make your situation a whole lot worse by restoring the "wrong" data, trust me.

Tip   Your database must have either full recovery model or bulk-logged recovery model enabled in order to have transaction logs to restore.

Transaction Log Restore Fundamentals

There are a few basic things that we need to get out of the way when dealing with transaction log restores in the context of this chapter. First of all, I am not going to get into the weeds of what transaction logs are and how they work or what data is present at which bit and why that is important. To me, that is a subject is probably best left out of this particular book, because I want this book to be more closely related to solving a problem as opposed to learning the subtleties of a problem. Having said that, let's just go over a few small topics that I feel are important (and maybe a few that aren't but could still relate to the overall issue of transaction log restorations).

There are two ways to restore a transaction log: either using SSMS, or using Transact-SQL. Yes, it could be argued that both ways use Transact-SQL, since that is the language of SQL Server, but I am referring specifically to using SQL Server Management Studio to create a SQL Server Agent job to automate the restoration, or manually using Transact-SQL either from a CLI or also within SSMS.

For the next section, I executed what is shown in Listing 7-1 in SSMS.

Listing 7-1. Create More Data for the Database

```
DECLARE @cnt INT;
SET @cnt = 0;

WHILE @cnt <= 1000
BEGIN
        INSERT INTO users1 SELECT * FROM users2;
        SET @cnt = @cnt + 1;
END;

SELECT count(*) as cnt FROM users1;
```

This is an excerpt of CreateTestData.sql that we created back in Chapter 1. My record count before I ran this excerpt was 10,020,000, and the record count after I ran this excerpt was 20,030,000. That should make for a pretty substantial difference in size of the transaction log.

What I want to do is restore to the previous version of the database, where the record count was 10,020,000. The next section will detail how to do this in SQL Server Management Studio using the *Files and Filegroups* interface, and then a point-in-time restore using the *Restore Database* interface.

Restoring Using SSMS

The simplest way to run a restoration is probably graphically. I'm sure there will be some old-school command-line gurus that will point out the error in my ways, and to them I simply say, "Hey, wow, you did essentially the same thing in a console that I did in a GUI... sweet." And that's about it. I'm not one of those developers that prescribes to a specific methodology, whether GUI (in SSMS) or CLI (using Transact-SQL). I prefer to use whatever tool is available and I don't really care to get too far into the dichotomy of "you should use this tool because it's so fantastic and any

other way is terrible." For example, I write ColdFusion in Dreamweaver.
I don't use ColdFusion Builder, the IDE specifically built for ColdFusion
development. Why? Because I initially preferred the layout and structure
of Dreamweaver over CF Builder, and even after all these years, I still do.
That doesn't mean that ColdFusion Builder is any worse or better than
Dreamweaver; it just means that my personal preference is for one over the
other, and I am sure I am not alone when having preferences for certain
software tools over others.

If you were to go straight into the menu structure with the thought in
mind that "I want to restore a transaction log," you may start with the Tasks
menu option after right-clicking the database name. Figure 7-1 shows this
starting point.

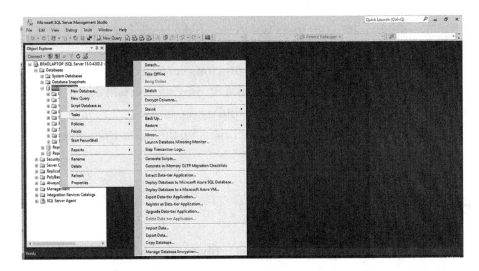

Figure 7-1. *Tasks submenu*

From here, it is a logical assumption that you would point to the
Restore area to the right, and proceed from there. This is correct, but the
next part is where it could be confusing. Figure 7-2 shows the expanded
menu of the Restore selection.

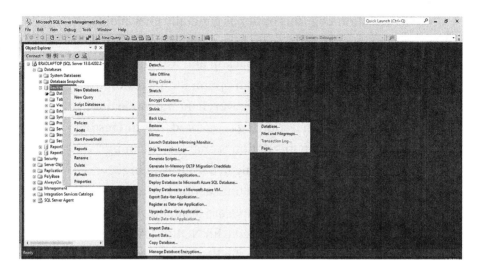

Figure 7-2. *Restore menu selections*

This menu has four options. Those options are as follows:

- Database: This option will allow you to restore a database from either a full or a differential backup. This option will not allow you to restore a transaction log.

- Files and Filegroups: This option will allow you to restore a group of files to a new or existing database. You have the option of selecting a full or differential backup, and the corresponding transaction logs will be selected for the restore operation. Consequently, you can choose an individual transaction log to restore, and your selection will automatically include every transaction log since the last full or differential backup. Note that all current backups are included in this interface, so be very careful when restoring data.

- Transaction Log: This option is generally unavailable, except in a few certain situations. When a database has been restored using a full backup and RESTORE WITH STANDBY was selected as an option for the restoration, the database will stay in RecoveryPending mode until the tail of the transaction log is restored. It is interesting to note that, when this option is enabled, meaning that the database is currently in a state awaiting restoration of the tail of the transaction log, all three remaining options in this area are disabled. Also, when a database has been restored with NORECOVERY and the database is currently in the Restoring... mode, this option is available and means that you can continue to restore transaction logs.

- Page: This option will let you check your database pages for possible corruption, and also let you restore from the most current backup set of full, differential, and transaction log backups. Your selection must comprise a complete backup set, which will represent a complete restore solution.

For the purpose of this demonstration, we are going to choose the Files and Filegroups option. This will give us some options we need to restore our transaction log. You can open the Files and Filegroups window by right-clicking the database you want to work with and navigating to Tasks ➤ Restore ➤ File and Filegroups. Figure 7-3 shows the location of this menu option.

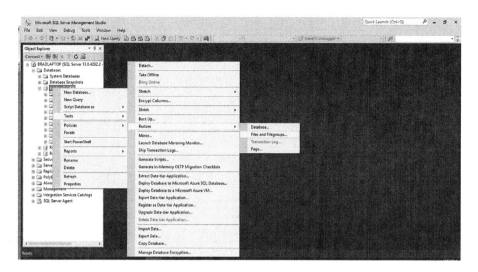

Figure 7-3. *Files and Filegroups menu location*

Restore Files and Filegroups—General

Figure 7-4 shows the initial interface for the Restore Files and Filegroups section. Notice that, by default, the selected page is General, as indicated on the left of the interface.

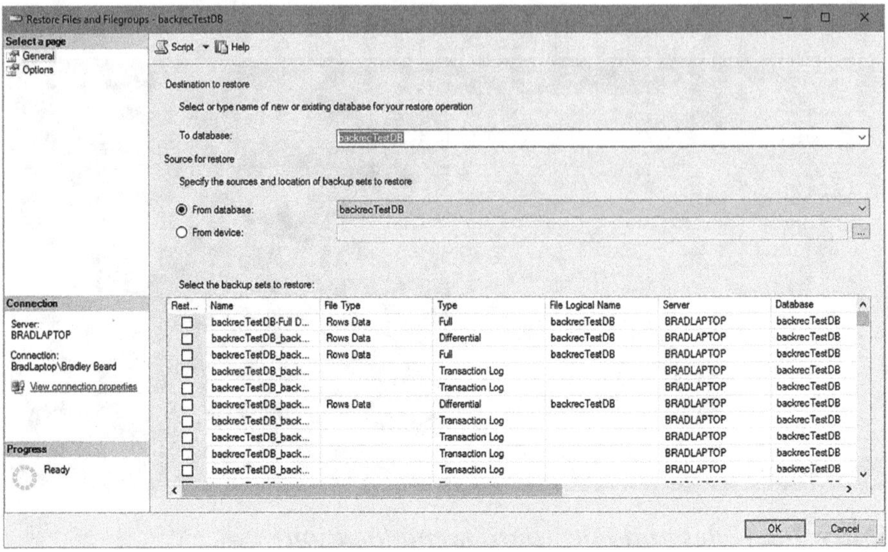

Figure 7-4. *Restore Files and Filegroups, General page*

Let's take a minute to get familiar with this screen. The general interface is nearly the same as quite a few other general screens in SQL Server, meaning that there is a destination field along with a source field. This tells the user that there are generally both sides of the equation to fill in, and both sets of data have to be filled out and correct if the equation is going to balance out and render the expected results.

The first section, *Destination to restore,* carries the names of the databases with full or bulk-logged recovery models. Your database should be selected by default.

The second section, *Source for restore,* carries the names of the databases that have viable backups available for restoring.

Underneath these two options, the backup sets are shown. The initial layout has the following columns shown:

- Restore: Check box value for yes or no; checked for yes, unchecked for no.

- Name: The name of the backup file. Note that the file extension is not included in this view.

- File Type: This value is "Rows Data" for either full or differential backups, or blank for transaction log backups.

- Type: The type of the backup; values are full, differential, or transaction log.

- File Logical Name: The logical name of the file, apart from the Name field.

- Server: This is the name of the SQL Server instance the backup was run from.

- Database: This is the name of the SQL Server database that the backup originated from.

- Start Date: The date and time when the backup operation started.

- Finish Date: The date and time the backup operation finished.

- Size: The size of the backup.

- Username: The username of the account used to generate the backup.

You will use these columns to determine exactly which backups to restore and the order in which to restore them. Luckily, SSMS makes this easy for you.

Scroll down to the bottom of the *Select the backup sets to restore:* area. The last item listed in this area should be a transaction log backup. If a transaction log isn't listed last, then move up the list, or earlier in time, to the last transaction log backup. Check the Restore check box and notice that all the other transaction logs since the last differential backup become selected, along with the last differential backup. This is because SQL Server is aware that it needs to restore a full backup first, then the differential backup, and then the transaction logs, in the correct time order, in order to successfully restore the database to the point in time. You should see something similar to what is shown in Figure 7-5 at this point.

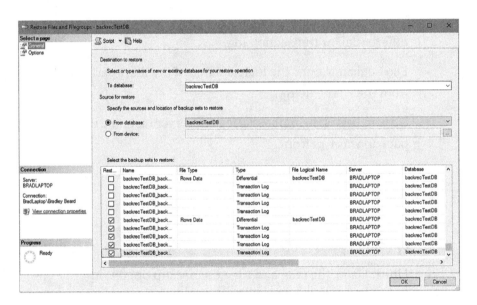

Figure 7-5. *Last transaction log selected*

Notice that the options selected are four transaction log backups and one differential backup, as indicated by the Type column.

Restore Files and Filegroups—Options

The second page, referenced from the left of the interface shown in Figure 7-6, is titled Options.

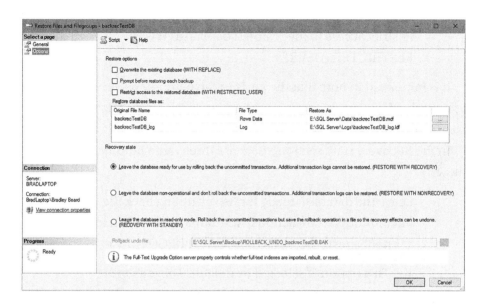

Figure 7-6. *Restore Files and Filegroups, Options page*

In this area, we see a few options that can be a bit offputting if you aren't already familiar with them. Let's go over them before we move on.

There are two main sections of this interface: *Restore options* and *Recovery state*. The *Restore options* section allows you to customize the various options available to you, the DBA, before the data restore process begins and while the process executes, while the Recovery state section allows you to define what happens after the data has been restored.

In the Restore options section, there are three check boxes, titled as follows:

- Overwrite the existing database (WITH REPLACE)

- Prompt before restoring each backup

- Restrict access to the restored database (WITH RESTRICTED_USER)

It is important to note that the parts in the parentheses are the pieces to remember if you ever restore a backup using Transact-SQL, which is discussed in the next section.

In the Recovery state section, there are three radio buttons, titled as follows:

- Leave the database ready for use by rolling back the uncommitted transactions. Additional transaction logs cannot be restored. (RESTORE WITH RECOVERY)

  - This option is selected by default. The reason is because this is the most common use for backup recovery; to leave the database ready to run immediately by rolling back any uncommitted transactions.

- Leave the database nonoperational and don't roll back the uncommitted transactions. Additional transaction logs can be restored. (RESTORE WITH NONRECOVERY)

  - This is the most destructive option. I honestly can't imagine a scenario where I would want a production database nonoperational, unless we're dealing with failovers or load balancing. In that case, yes, I could imagine this being useful to repair the database instance, but other than that, like I said, it's destructive because the database is left nonoperational until the database is explicitly brought back online.

- Leave the database in read-only mode. Roll back the uncommitted transactions but save the rollback operation in a file so the recovery effects can be undone. (RECOVERY WITH STANDBY)

  - This option lets you essentially "pause" the database and put it in read-only mode. The uncommitted transactions get rolled back, but the rollbacks are saved so that they can be undone later, if needed. This would be a good option for ensuring that everything is working as intended in the database, for example.

  - Choosing this option lets you select a location for a rollback undo file.

For a "regular" backup, meaning that you just want to restore data to the last transaction log backup, all you need to restore is the last differential backup, and then the transaction logs, in order, up to the point in time that you need to access data from. For the large majority of restores, this is the case.

It is very rare that you will want to restore to a specific point in time many days ago, and run the risk of losing all data accumulated after that point, in other words. There have been specific instances where this is exactly the case though, and in this case, I would strongly recommend running a current backup of the database before doing *anything* to a production or development database. After a backup has run and has been verified, then proceed with whatever path you want to take to restore the database. In my experience, I have found that it is beneficial to restore the full, differential, and transaction log backups to a secondary database for verification of the data being sought. Once the data is found, I then create *INSERT INTO... SELECT* scripts to update my primary database from my secondary database. Once the update is complete and I have verified that my data has been recovered successfully, I can drop the secondary database and continue on with my day. The only caveat I have to stress is to ensure that the *INSERT INTO... SELECT* statements are properly written to update the primary database from the secondary database correctly; otherwise, you're just creating more work for yourself.

I find this to be a fantastic method to ensure that the data between the primary and secondary database tables being restored is correct, since I am outside of the current primary database but working on an exact duplicate in the secondary database from a point in time.

To continue, just ensure that the *Overwrite the existing database (WITH REPLACE)* option is checked and that the transaction log (roll up to the previous full backup) before the data update is selected, and click the OK button. Figure 7-7 shows the window that tells us that our database was successfully restored.

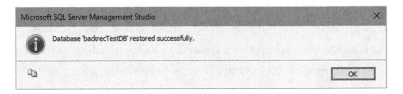

Figure 7-7. *Database restored successfully*

Click OK on this window and notice that our main Restore Files and Filegroups window has closed. Go back over to SSMS and run the following query:

```
SELECT count(*) as cnt FROM users1
```

Your result should be 10,020,000. Congratulations!

Point-in-Time Restore/Recovery

In order to restore a transaction log, we first need to restore a full backup and optionally a differential backup. Have you ever seen the state of a database in SSMS when a database is stuck in Restoring mode? As I noted earlier in this chapter, that happens when a database has been restored with a full or differential backup with the RESTORE WITH STANDBY or RESTORE WITH NORECOVERY option selected. It will stay in the Restoring state until the tail of the transaction log is restored or the RESTORE WITH RECOVERY statement is executed as part of a restore process. Let's take a look at this in practice.

In SQL Server Management Studio, right-click your database (mine is named backrecTestDB) and navigate to Tasks ➤ Restore ➤ Database... to continue. Figure 7-8 shows the location of this menu item.

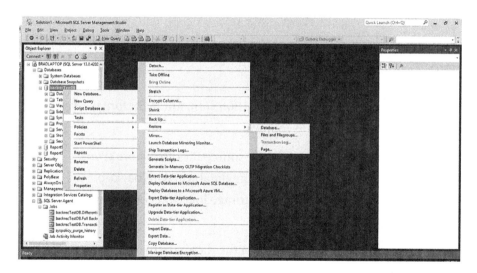

Figure 7-8. *Restore Database menu location*

The interface that opens is titled *Restore Database*. Note that there are three tabs on the left titled *General, Files,* and *Options* for different pages within this interface. The default selection is *General,* which is what we see in Figure 7-9.

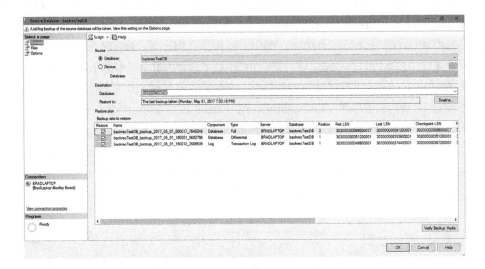

Figure 7-9. *Restore Database interface*

This page shows us a *Source,* a *Destination,* and a *Restore plan* section. These sections are defined as follows:

- Source: The location of the source files to restore **from**. This can be either an existing database with backup files or a local or network storage location containing backup files.

- Destination: The location of the database to restore **to**. The default for the *Restore to* field here is for the last backup set, but that can be adjusted by clicking the Timeline… button and choosing a timeframe to restore from. This is referred to as a *point-in-time restore*.

- Restore plan: The section details the files that will be restored, and the *Backup sets to restore:* section, which is covered shortly.

Let's say that I wanted to restore my database to the state it was in at 8:00 this morning. This section of the interface is where you want to go for that, because this section allows you to pinpoint a specific time and data to restore data from.

Click the *Timeline* button shown in the *Destination* section of the interface shown in Figure 7-9. A screen opens as shown in Figure 7-10 that is titled *Backup Timeline: backrecTestDB* (or whatever your database is named).

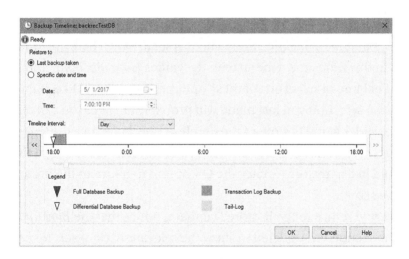

Figure 7-10. *Backup Timeline: backrecTestDB*

Notice that the initial configuration is for *Last backup taken.* In this case, the time of the last backup taken was 7:00 PM. This might be ideal for you, but I want to restore to 8:00 AM, remember? Click the radio button for *Specific date and time* and select the date you want to restore to. Figure 7-11 shows my updated interface.

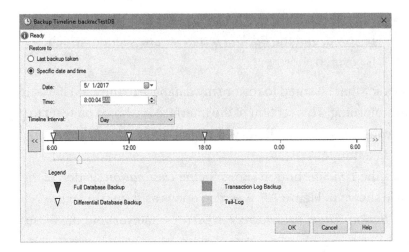

Figure 7-11. *Backup Timeline: backrecTestDB, updated*

Notice that the *Timeline Interval* field is set to *Day*. There are other options in this drop-down menu with the values *Hour, Six hour,* and *Week* as well. Feel free to select any of these options, if you would like, but the value of the selection you just made will probably change. You can also move the slider at the bottom of the timeline view but above the legend for a more precise timeline location. When you have selected the right time you would like to restore to, click the OK button to return to the Restore Database screen.

Once you return to the Restore Database, notice that the *Backup sets to restore:* section has updated to show the relevant backup sets to restore. Typically, this area will be populated by the full and differential backups which relate to the selected timeframe of the transactions needing to be restored. Figure 7-12 shows my screen after the *Backup sets to restore:* section has been repopulated.

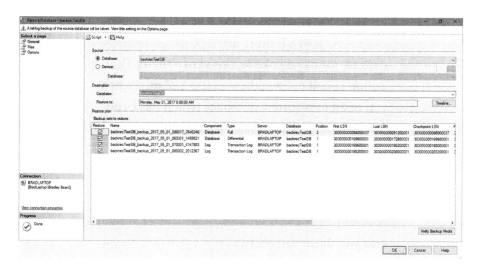

Figure 7-12. *Restore Database, updated*

At this point, we can see the full backup at the top of the list, followed by the differential backup, and the two transaction log backups at the bottom. Click the *Verify Backup Media* button if you would like to verify the media; I generally click this button anytime I see it, just in case.

The Files tab on the left can be left alone for now. This is where you would normally define where the restored files will be stored and what their names will be, but we are not going to change this setting.

The Options tab needs some explanation. Go ahead and navigate there, and notice that the interface has the following sections and selections:

- Restore options

  - Overwrite the existing database (WITH REPLACE): This option overwrites the database files for the selected database. This is a very destructive option, so use it at your own risk.

155

- Preserve the replication settings (WITH KEEP_ REPLICATION): If there are replication settings defined for the database, then keep them. This option specifically addresses the instance when you need to restore a database which has been published to a different server than the server the database was backed up on.

- Restrict access to the restored database (WITH RESTRICTED_USER): Once the database is restored, only the members of db_owner, dbcreator, and sysadmin can access.

- Recovery state

- RESTORE WITH RECOVERY: This option will restore all the backup sets as the default.

- RESTORE WITH NORECOVERY: This option will leave the database in the Restoring... state discussed earlier. Once the tail of the transaction log has been restored, the database will then move to a normal state.

- RESTORE WITH STANDBY: This option will leave the database in a read-only state. If this option is chosen, you must specify a Standby file.

- Standby file: This file will reverse the recovery effort.

- Tail-log backup (a backup that contains the portion of the transaction log not previously backed up, or the active portion of the transaction log)

  - Take tail-log backup before restore: Specifies that you would like to back up the tail of the transaction log.

- Leave source database in the restoring state
  (WITH NORECOVERY): Same as the option
  listed previously; the database will be left in the
  Restoring... state.

- Backup file: The location of the backup file for the
  tail of the transaction log.

- Server connections

  - Close existing connections to destination database:
    Basically, this option puts the database into
    single-user mode and closes all connections to
    the database engine from SSMS. Once the restore
    process is complete, the database is put back
    to multiuser mode and connections are made
    available again.

- Prompt

  - Prompt before restoring each backup: This option
    will show a pop-up window asking if you want to
    proceed with each restore.

For this Options tab, I only want to check *Overwrite the existing database* and uncheck *Leave source database in the restoring state*. Everything else can stay the same on this screen (Figure 7-13).

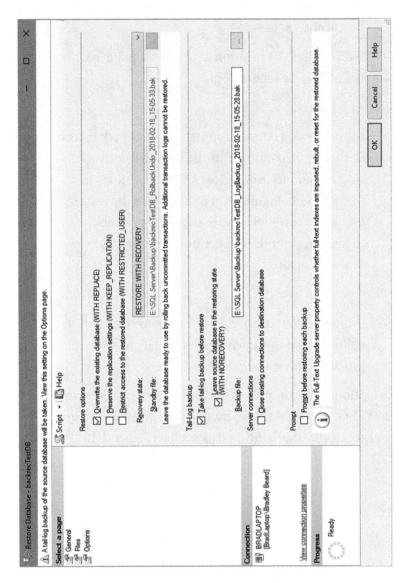

Figure 7-13. Restore Database, Options tab

When you are ready, click the OK button at the bottom of the screen. You should see the standard "Restoring" section at the top of the interface and a progressive percentage going up to 100% until it successfully completes.

Next, go back over to SSMS and run the following query:

```
SELECT count(*) as cnt FROM users1
```

Your result should be 20030000. Congratulations!

In this first section, we have successfully restored transaction logs two different ways within SQL Server Management Studio.

Restoring Using Transact-SQL

This method is a bit easier. In the download of SQL Server Management Studio, there is a sidebar available titled Template Browser. If you don't see it immediately available, press Ctrl+Alt+T, or go to View ➤ Template Explorer in SSMS. The sidebar should open to the right of the main window. Scroll down to the Restore submenu and expand it. You should see Restore Database and Restore Files and Filegroups as files under the Restore submenu. This should look familiar, because we just dealt with these interfaces in the previous section.

The general idea goes like this: you double-click whichever template you want to edit, and the template opens up as a new query in the main SSMS window. You can then make whatever changes you want to this file and save it to your local file system as a brand-new script.

Restore File and Filegroups Template

This template is a bit more involved than the Restore Database template introduced shortly, and for good reason. This template deals with restoring individual files, whereas the Restore Database template simply restores the database and that's it. First things first; we need to delete the portion of the template that wants us to create a database, back up the database, and back up the transaction log. This essentially means that we are going to delete lines 5 through 41, inclusive. That means we should be left with four statements, each beginning with RESTORE. Next, we want to delete one of these RESTORE statements. The reason for this is because we are assuming that we are going to restore a full backup, then a differential backup, and then the transaction log.

Before we go any further, let's add some more data to the database by running the script shown in Listing 7-2. Note that this is exactly the same script as Listing 7-1.

Listing 7-2. Create More Data for the Database

```
DECLARE @cnt INT;
SET @cnt = 0;

WHILE @cnt <= 1000
BEGIN
        INSERT INTO users1 SELECT * FROM users2;
        SET @cnt = @cnt + 1;
END;
```

The record count before running this script was 20030000, and the record count after running the script is 30040000. Now that this data is in the table, go ahead and run a full backup and a differential backup using the SQL Server Agent jobs you should have created in Chapter 1.

Next, you should modify your script to look like what is shown in Listing 7-3.

Listing 7-3. Restore Script

```
USE master

-- full database restore
RESTORE DATABASE backrecTestDB
        FROM DISK = N'E:\SQL Server\Backup\backrecTestDB_FULL.bak'
        WITH NORECOVERY, REPLACE

-- differential database restore
RESTORE DATABASE backrecTestDB
        FROM DISK = N'E:\SQL Server\Backup\backrecTestDB_
        DIFFERENTIAL.bak'
        WITH NORECOVERY

-- Restore logs
-- restore 7 AM log
RESTORE LOG backrecTestDB
        FROM DISK = N'E:\SQL Server\Logs\backrecTestDB_7AM.trn'
        WITH NORECOVERY

-- restore 8 AM log
RESTORE LOG backrecTestDB
        FROM DISK = N'E:\SQL Server\Logs\backrecTestDB_8AM.trn'
        WITH NORECOVERY

RESTORE DATABASE backrecTestDB WITH RECOVERY
```

Executing the script shown in Listing 7-2 in SQL Server Management Studio will render what is shown in Figure 7-14.

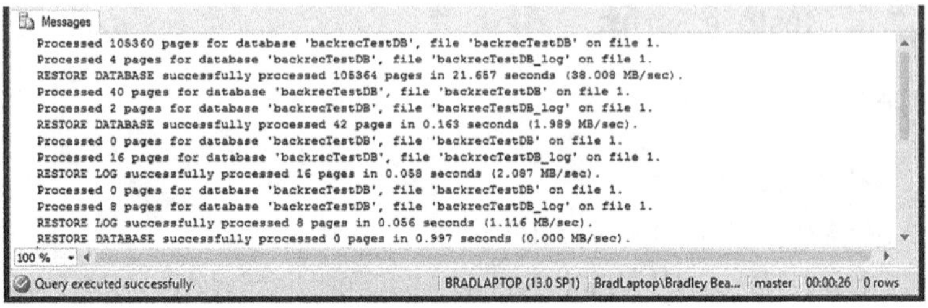

Figure 7-14. *Script results*

We can see there that the full, differential, and transaction log backups have been successfully restored. The record count before running this script was 30,040,000, and the record count after running the script is 20,030,000.

So there we have it! We have successfully restored transaction logs using SQL Server Management Studio and Transact-SQL.

Summary

In this chapter, we have learned how the various parts of the restoration process within SQL Server work together to create a viable solution for restoring data. We looked at the different parts of the interfaces necessary within SQL Server Management Studio to complete the task.

The final script for the transaction log restore is available as TransactionLogRestore.sql in the download for this book.

In the next chapter, we are going to tie together all of the restoration principles we have learned in Chapters 5 through 8 into one giant restoration script.

CHAPTER 8

Restore Solution Examples

In this chapter, we will tie together what we have learned from Chapters 5 through 7 into a cohesive structure that we can use to create a typical restore scenario. Note that we have not yet touched on all concepts of restoring data in the previous chapters; that will be remedied in this chapter, since I will focus more on the various conditions and options that are shown on the various screens in SSMS and that are available from using `sqlcmd`. This chapter will therefore be more of an all-encompassing look at every angle of restoring data within SQL Server, from the basic full restore to the exact point in time of the transaction log restore.

One of the most important things to keep in mind when setting up a restore scenario is that you need to practice implementing it before it gets put into a production environment. You should have step-by-step instructions on how to execute the restore, and they should be simple enough that a non-DBA will be able to sit down at a server console and successfully execute the restore scenario. I know that this seems like a daunting task, but I will help you write this procedure at the end of this chapter.

The first thing that we must do to enforce a restore scenario is define the criteria for restoration. We need to come up with a set of situations which would require a restore, and then define which type of restore would be

© Bradley Beard 2018
B. Beard, *Beginning Backup and Restore for SQL Server*,
https://doi.org/10.1007/978-1-4842-3456-3_8

best suited to that situation. It's very easy to just say to restore to the latest point in the transaction log, because this is probably true for 99% of the situations that we will encounter as DBAs. There are situations when this is not the best approach though, and that is what we need to prepare for.

Let's define a few situations and then the appropriate restore types that we need for each situation. In these scenarios, we want to

- transfer the production database to the development environment for testing

- recover from a catastrophic error at an unknown point in the previous evening

- recover data that was overwritten 15 minutes ago

- make a backup outside of the regular backup schedule that we can use as a "known good starting point"

As you can see, for at least half of these, we can just restore from the last transaction log and be done with it. That is the advantage of restoring data (besides actually getting your data restored); for the most part, there really isn't a lot of forethought required to restore data. You know that the data resides in the backups, so restore the backups. Pretty straightforward, and from there, we can keep it as simple or make it as complicated as we need it to be.

Before we get into building a complete restore scenario, let's go over some topics that didn't really fit into the previous chapters and certainly deserve a spot when discussing restoration of data. Not all restorations are done from the database option in Object Explorer, when we would right-click the database name, hover over Tasks, then Restore, then select the database option. There are two other options in this menu that we haven't discussed, and those options are "Files and Filegroups" and "Page." What this means is that we can not only restore from the database, but also restore the individual files and filegroups, or down to the page level.

Page Restores

With page restores, the important thing to remember is that the suspect_ pages table in the msdb database is where the possible corruption information lives. The structure of this table is shown in Table 8-1.

Table 8-1. *msdb..suspect_pages Structure*

Column Name	Description
database_id	ID of the database with the corruption.
file_id	ID of the file in the corrupted database.
page_id	ID of the page that is suspected to be corrupted.
event_type	Number which represents the type of error. Possible values are as follows:
	1. This is the "catch-all" of error values. This means either an 823 (due to hardware fault) or 824 error (other database corruption) has occurred.
	2. Incorrect checksum.
	3. Torn page.
	4. Restored page (after being flagged as suspect).
	5. Repaired by DBCC (after being flagged as suspect).
	6. Deallocated by DBCC (after being flagged as suspect)
error_count	Count of the times that the error occurred.
last_update_date	Date and time of the entry.

There are a few things to keep in mind when wanting to perform page restores. For example, you can only restore database pages. That may seem obvious, but the implication is that you cannot restore transaction logs or any of the "special" pages: specifically, allocation pages, global allocation map pages, shared global allocation map pages, and page free space pages. Microsoft uses very precise language when they say "only database pages" at `https://docs.microsoft.com/en-us/sql/relational-databases/ backup-restore/restore-pages-sql-server`, in other words.

Querying msdb..suspect_pages

The `msdb..suspect_pages` table holds the key to telling you which pages are suspected to be corrupt, which will hopefully lead you to a solid plan to restore those corrupted pages. There probably isn't anything really damaging yet, but there could be in the future, in other words.
A lot of times, the database can be repaired by general database restore operations, which overwrite pages by default. In the case of a database being restored, it is important to realize that, if the corrupted page has been backed up to the backup set being restored, then the corrupted data will remain until it is fixed.

Open up a New Query window and type `SELECT * FROM msdb.. suspect_pages;` and press F5 on your keyboard. When I run this query, I get zero results returned, which is a good thing. If I had gotten any results, I would take immediate action as shown in Table 8-2.

Table 8-2. *Page Restore Actions*

Step	Description
1	Get the page_id of the corrupted pages from the msdb..suspect_pages query output.

2	Start a page restore using a full backup, file backup, or filegroup backup which contains the corresponding corrupted page.
	If running from T-SQL and not SSMS, use the following syntax:
	
	`RESTORE DATABASE <database_id>`
	`PAGE = '<file_id: page_id>'`
	`FROM <backup device or file>`
	`WITH NORECOVERY`
	
	Note that the database_id, file_id, and page_id values all come from the msdb..suspect_pages query run earlier.

3	Restore the latest differential backup.
4	Restore the relevant transaction log backups.
5	Back up the tail of the transaction log.
6	Restore the transaction log from Step 5.

Following those steps will let you restore the page safely within T-SQL.

Complete Database Restore Using T-SQL

Recall that since we are working in the full recovery model, we have a lot more functionality at our disposal for backing up and restoring data. Particularly, we have granular control over how much or how little data we want to restore based on the current situation. The full recovery model allows us to restore the entire database, if needed, and more importantly, it can be restored to a specific point in time, as we saw in Chapter 5.

There is a basic set of instructions to follow when restoring a database in the full recovery model. The general set of instructions is shown in Listing 8-1.

Listing 8-1. Databasve Restore Instructions

- Switch to the master database

- Create a tail-log backup using `BACKUP LOG backrecTestDB TO DISK = 'E:\SQL Server\Logs\ backrecTestDB_TLOG_TAIL.bak' WITH NORECOVERY;`

  - SSMS Response: `Processed 18 pages for database 'backrecTestDB', file 'backrecTestDB_log' on file 1. BACKUP LOG successfully processed 18 pages in 0.069 seconds (1.981 MB/sec).`

- Restore the latest full backup using `RESTORE DATABASE backrecTestDB FROM DISK = 'E:\SQL Server\ Backup\backrecTestDB_FULL.BAK' WITH NORECOVERY;`

  - SSMS Response: `Processed 107968 pages for database 'backrecTestDB', file 'backrecTestDB' on file 1. Processed 2 pages for database 'backrecTestDB', file 'backrecTestDB_log' on file 1. RESTORE DATABASE successfully processed 107970 pages in 21.669 seconds (38.927 MB/sec).`

- Restore the latest differential backup using `RESTORE DATABASE backrecTestDB FROM DISK = 'E:\SQL Server\Backup\backrecTestDB_DIFF.BAK' WITH NORECOVERY;`

- SSMS Response: `Processed 136 pages for database 'backrecTestDB', file 'backrecTestDB' on file 1. Processed 2 pages for database 'backrecTestDB', file 'backrecTestDB_log' on file 1. RESTORE DATABASE successfully processed 138 pages in 0.283 seconds (3.795 MB/sec).`

- Restore the oldest transaction log backup from the latest differential backup using `RESTORE LOG backrecTestDB FROM DISK = 'E:\SQL Server\Logs\backrecTestDB_backup_2017_10_16_190004_6842741.trn' WITH NORECOVERY;`

  - SSMS Response: `Processed 0 pages for database 'backrecTestDB', file 'backrecTestDB' on file 1. Processed 16 pages for database 'backrecTestDB', file 'backrecTestDB_log' on file 1. RESTORE LOG successfully processed 16 pages in 0.059 seconds (2.118 MB/sec).`

- Continue restoring transaction log backups until you recover to the point of failure

  - SSMS Response: `Processed 0 pages for database 'backrecTestDB', file 'backrecTestDB' on file 1. Processed 8 pages for database 'backrecTestDB', file 'backrecTestDB_log' on file 1. RESTORE LOG successfully processed 8 pages in 0.047 seconds (1.329 MB/sec).`

- Recover the database using RESTORE DATABASE
  backrecTestDB WITH RECOVERY;

  - SSMS Response: RESTORE DATABASE successfully
    processed 0 pages in 0.873 seconds (0.000 MB/sec).

Note that I am using false names in the DISK attributes of these
instructions. This is so it is easier for you to understand which backup I am
looking for in a set of backups.

If you notice in the SSMS Response bullets in Listing 8-1, in the
transaction log restore portion, I restored the first log after the differential
backup was restored, and then I restored the next log after that, which is
when I got the message that 0 pages were processed, which means that I'm
at the end of the applicable transaction logs. Now, there could be more to
be restored after this log was restored, but in this case, that is the end of the
data that needed to be restored. In a real-world scenario, you would have a
specific time of day that you would need to restore data to so keep in mind
that you may need to restore more logs than are shown in the example.
Simply rewrite the script for the transaction log restores that you need.

With these instructions in mind, a good restore script can be pieced
together as shown in Listing 8-2.

Listing 8-2. Restore Script

```
-- switch to master database
USE master
GO

-- backup the tail of the log
BACKUP LOG backrecTestDB
TO DISK = 'E:\SQL Server\Logs\backrecTestDB_TLOG_TAIL.bak'
WITH NORECOVERY;
GO
```

```
-- restore the Full backup
RESTORE DATABASE backrecTestDB FROM DISK = 'E:\SQL Server\
Backup\backrecTestDB_backup_2017_10_16_000002_2492163.bak'
WITH NORECOVERY;
GO

-- restore the Differential backup
RESTORE DATABASE backrecTestDB FROM DISK = 'E:\SQL Server\
Backup\backrecTestDB_backup_2017_10_16_180001_7394135.bak'
WITH NORECOVERY;
GO

-- restore the Transaction Log backups
RESTORE LOG backrecTestDB FROM DISK = 'E:\SQL Server\Logs\
backrecTestDB_backup_2017_10_16_190004_6842741.trn'
WITH NORECOVERY;
GO

RESTORE LOG backrecTestDB FROM DISK = 'E:\SQL Server\Logs\
backrecTestDB_backup_2017_10_16_200001_9609626.trn'
WITH NORECOVERY;
GO

RESTORE DATABASE backrecTestDB WITH RECOVERY;
GO
```

Once you have run the script shown in Listing 8-2, you can always run the script shown in Listing 8-3 to verify that your database is back online.

Listing 8-3. Database Status Verification

```
SELECT databasepropertyex ('backrecTestDB', 'Status');
```

171

That should return just the value ONLINE in the Results page of SSMS. Once you see this, then you can be assured that everything has been restored successfully and your database is running smoothly.

Complete Database Restore Using SSMS

The process for restoring a database using SSMS is exactly the same as using T-SQL; we just aren't going to write the code to do it. We are going to let the interface do the work for us.

Figure 8-1 shows what my tables look like in Object Explorer pane before we do anything.

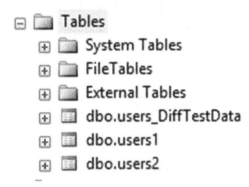

Figure 8-1. *Current tables*

What we want to do is create a situation where I need to restore the entire database, and then walk through the process of restoring the backups in order from full to differential to transaction logs. A fun way to do this is to just drop a table or two. That's pretty much a great reason to run a restore operation, right? When you're ready, first verify that you have a current set of database backups that you can definitely restore from. Next, right-click a table or two and select Delete. This window is shown in Figure 8-2.

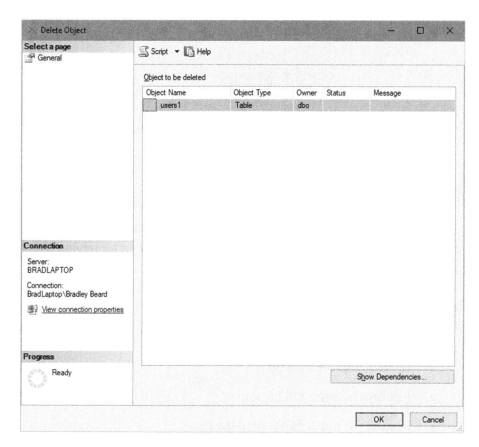

Figure 8-2. *Delete Object window*

There is only the one tab labeled General in this window. In the center pane, we can see that I have selected the users1 table to be deleted. When ready, just click OK and the table will be deleted.

Notice how my Object Explorer window no longer shows the users1 table, and I cannot query the table as well. Figure 8-3 shows my updated Object Explorer.

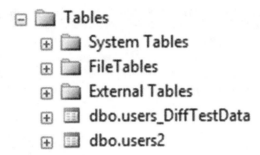

Figure 8-3. *Object Explorer, updated*

We are going to use the same sequence of events as when we restored using T-SQL. That sequence is shown in Listing 8-1 and an abbreviated version is repeated in Listing 8-4.

Listing 8-4. Restore Sequence

- Switch to the master database

- Create a tail-log backup

- Restore the latest full backup

- Restore the latest differential backup

- Restore the oldest transaction log backup from the latest differential backup

- Continue restoring transaction log backups until you recover to the point of failure

- Recover the database

Note that I have left out the specific SQL statements, since we won't need them in SSMS.

We need to connect to the `master` database to continue. We can either open a New Query window and select `master` from the Available Databases menu (or press Ctrl+U and the up and down arrow keys), or we can verify that we are connecting to the `master` database when we log in. If you are not connecting to `master` when you log in, you probably should consider changing. You can change your default database in the Connect to Server dialog shown in Figure 8-4.

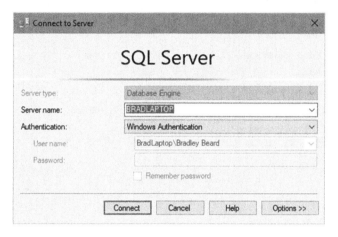

Figure 8-4. *Connect to Server*

Click the Options ➤ button and you will get an expanded interface, as shown in Figure 8-5.

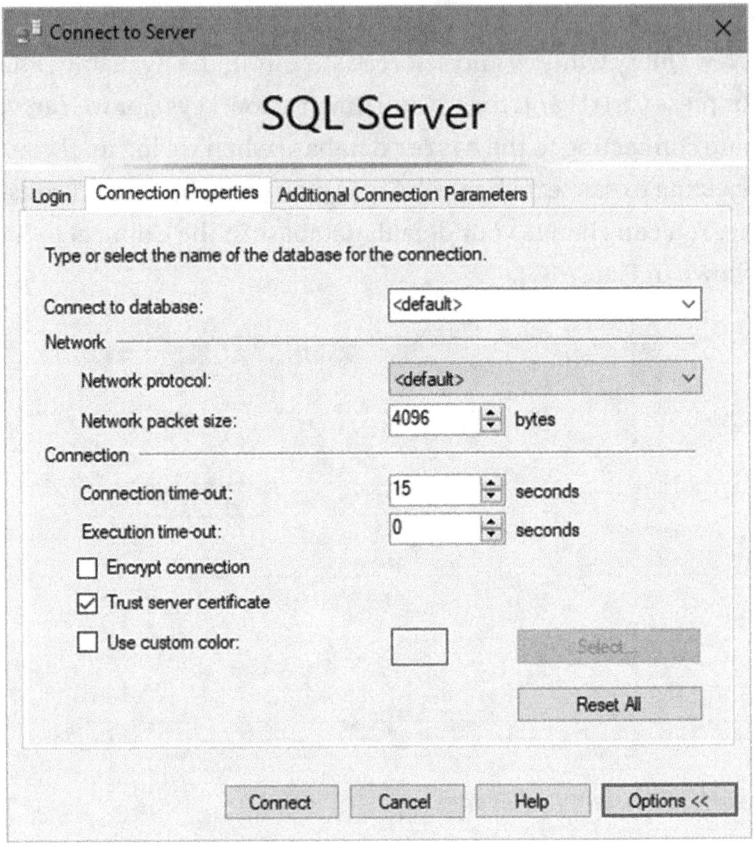

Figure 8-5. *Connect to server, expanded*

Pull down the drop-down menu next to Connect to database and select Browse server. A brief message pops up asking to connect to the server, so click the Yes button when you see this message. You are then shown the Browse Server for Database window, as shown in Figure 8-6.

Figure 8-6. *Browse Server for Database*

All we need to do here is select master and click OK, and master then shows instead of default in the Connect to Server window. Figure 8-7 shows my updated interface after choosing master.

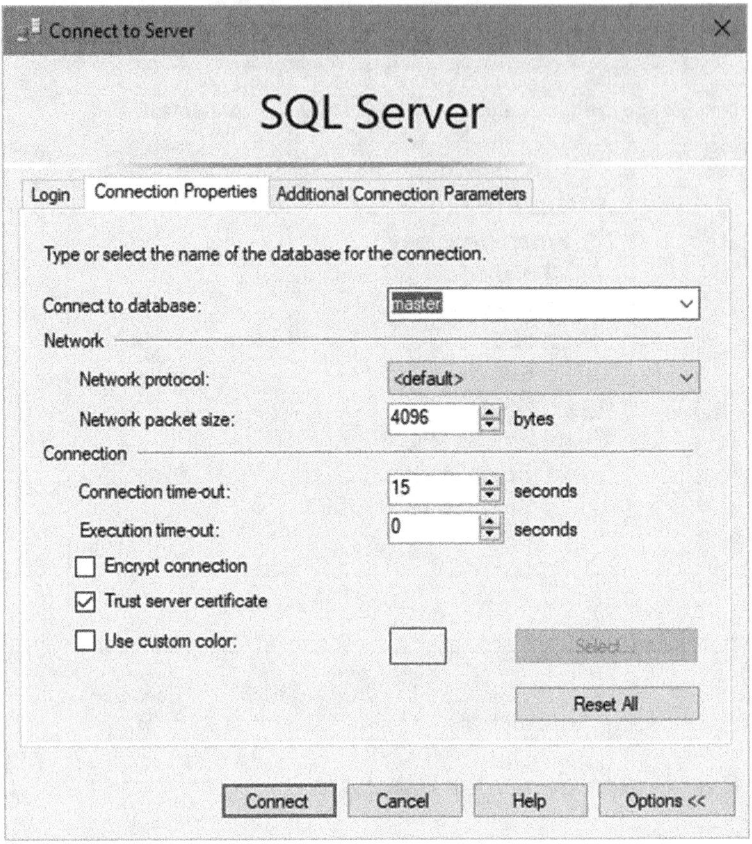

Figure 8-7. *Connect to Server, updated*

I have kept the rest of values in this and the other tabs at their default values. Once I press connect, I am then connected to the master database by default.

The next step is to take a backup of the transaction log. This is done by right-clicking the database name, hovering over Tasks, and then selecting Back Up. The location of this menu item is shown in Figure 8-8.

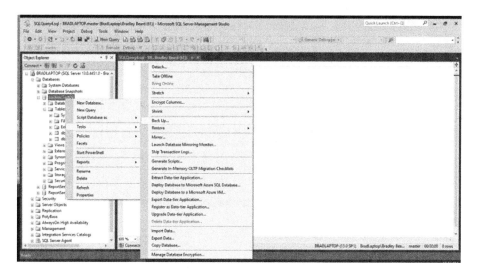

Figure 8-8. *Back Up location*

This opens up the Back Up Database screen, as shown in Figure 8-9. This default screen would be ideal if I wanted to run a full backup, as indicated by the backup type option of full, but I do not want to do this at this time.

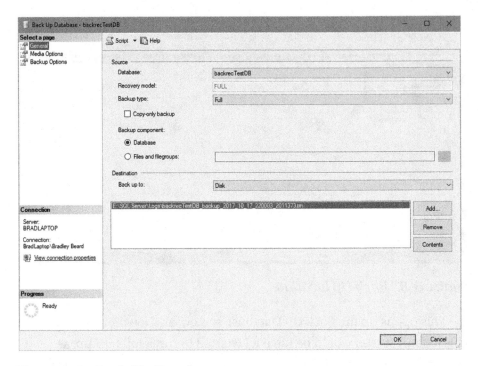

Figure 8-9. *Back Up Database*

Since I don't want to run a full backup, I need to pull that menu down and select transaction log instead. Once you make this change, you will see what is shown in Figure 8-10.

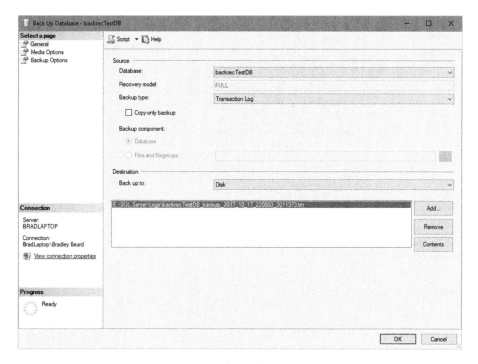

Figure 8-10. *Transaction Log selected*

This sets us up to back up our transaction log, but we aren't done yet. If we were to press OK here, we would be selecting the default values on the other tabs, and we haven't looked at those options yet.

Click the Media Options label on the left to show the Media Options screen. Figure 8-11 shows the default values for this screen.

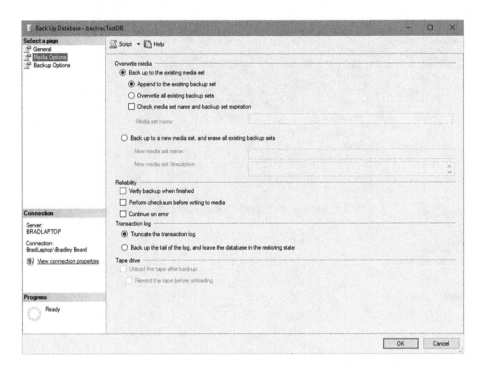

Figure 8-11. *Back Up Database, Media Options tab*

Note that the Truncate the transaction log radio button is selected in the transaction log section. This means that the default option is just to truncate and leave that ragged edge as the new tail of the transaction log. We want to leave this option as is. This is because we want to leave the database online and not in the restoring state. Select the specified option and press OK to continue. We don't need to worry about the default values in the Backup Options tab, since those default values are what we need.

A success message should quickly appear, letting us know that our backup has completed successfully. Click OK when you see this, and the Back Up Database screen will close.

Now, our database is shown in Figure 8-12 as back online, as expected.

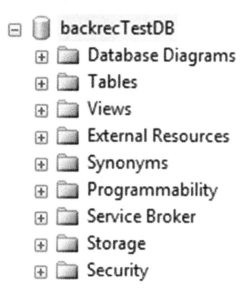

Figure 8-12. *Database is online*

Once we get here, we are ready to move to the next step in the operation and start the restoration of the data.

To begin a full database restore, we start much like before except with a slightly different menu location, as shown in Figure 8-13.

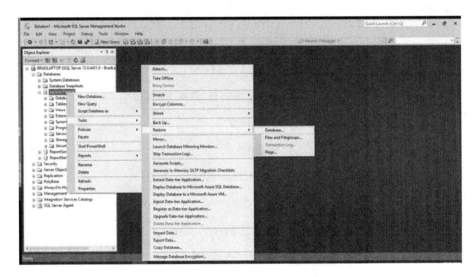

Figure 8-13. *Database menu location*

We are going to right-click our database and hover over Tasks, then Restore, and finally, select Database.

The default screen is shown in Figure 8-14. Note that this screen will automatically populate with a Restore Plan based on the latest backups of the selected database.

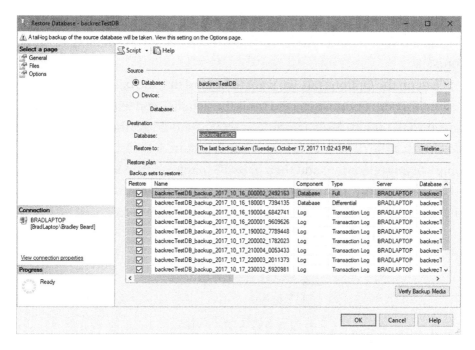

Figure 8-14. *Restore Database*

You can freely choose any of the options in the Database drop-down menu and watch how the backup sets values change with each selection.

Note   Notice how the Name field automatically defaults to show the full backup, then the differential backup, and then the transaction log backups since the last differential backup.

We want to choose the options in this area by default, since we want to restore the full, differential, and transaction log backups in the order they are shown in the interface. We want to be sure that we both wind back the transaction log and choose a point in time in the Timeline area or discount an entire transaction log. I am going to restore to the previous transaction log, since I know the data is resident in that backup.

185

The values in the Files tab are fine by default, since we don't want to rename any files. They are staying where they are going by default, in other words.

Over on the Options tab, we want to be sure that the tail-log backup section has both options selected (as is the default), and when we are ready, press the OK button. After a minute or so, you should get the message showing that the database was successfully restored. Click OK here to complete this operation, and then press F5 to refresh the SSMS interface.

Trust but verify, right? Go ahead and expand Tables under our database, and you should see what is shown in Figure 8-15.

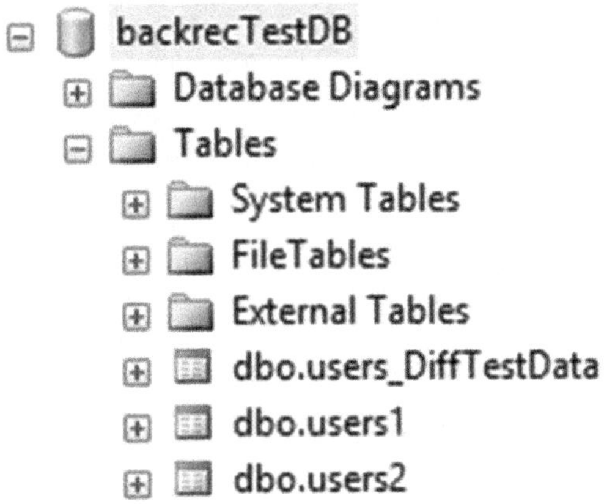

Figure 8-15. users1 returns!

So there you have it: a complete restore of a database using SSMS.

Database Snapshots

A great way to restore an entire database quickly is with database snapshots. This is a literal snapshot of a database at a particular moment in time, and is consistent with the actual database as of that moment in time. This means that the snapshot acts as a sort of duplicated database, because as the source database is updated, so is the snapshot. From the moment that the snapshot is taken, every subsequent transaction is captured in the snapshot as well as in the source database. You can also have multiple snapshots of the same database, which is a particularly good idea. This can be a great way to manage restoration of data, if managed correctly. For example, if the snapshot exists for a long time and is not dropped, it will continue to grow until it consumes the disk it resides on. This is clearly not ideal, and for this reason, snapshots must be maintained.

Let me pause here and mention that database snapshots are *never* to be used in place of a backup and restore scenario. If we aren't supposed to use them for backup or recovery, then what is their purpose? The main purpose for using database snapshots is for the DBA that wants to take a quick snapshot of their database, do something to the database that might mess up, and then test to make sure that the database change actually works. If it doesn't, then the DBA just restores the snapshot, and they are right back where they were a few minutes ago. The time to do this is generally much less than planning a restore operation and having to go through all the restore steps and figuring out which transaction logs to recover. Instead, just restore the snapshot and the job is complete.

Another good use for database snapshots is for reporting. With our naming convention, we can create a standard report that is based on data from the different snapshots taken during the day. This could be used for such purposes as tracking volume in sales, or monitoring the various transactions in dollars being recorded in the database throughout time. A rolling 24-hour window of data will be available to the reporting service, and quantifying this data into a dashboard for easy readability by management is a fantastic use of database snapshots. The topic of reporting in SQL Server is slightly outside of the scope of this book, so I recommend picking up Kathi Kellenberger's *Beginning SQL Server Reporting Services*, available at www.apress.com/us/book/9781484219898. This is an absolute necessity for those DBAs that are branching out into the world of SQL Server reporting services and don't quite know where to start.

How Does a Database Snapshot Work?

The concept of database snapshots can be somewhat intimidating to an unfamiliar user. The best way that I've heard it explained was that they are most closely related, in theory, to a static full database backup. The entire database as it existed at the time of creation resides as a read-only copy in this snapshot, and that one snapshot remains a read-only copy of the source database, up to the point that the snapshot is dropped.

Creating a Database Snapshot

Let's say that you have a SQL Server Agent job that will create a database snapshot every hour, and the oldest snapshot will be deleted after a certain number of snapshots is created. This is probably the most common usage scenario, because it limits the amount of data that is being stored in the snapshots, while still providing a reliable snapshot structure.

The syntax to create a database snapshot will be familiar to you, since it is essentially a CREATE DATABASE statement as shown in Listing 8-5.

Listing 8-5. Create Database Snapshot Syntax

```
CREATE DATABASE backrecTestDB_snapshot_12AM ON (
NAME = backrecTestDB,
FILENAME = 'E:\SQL Server\Data\backrecTestDB_data_12AM')
AS SNAPSHOT OF backrecTestDB;
```

The statement CREATE DATABASE backrecTestDB_snapshot_12AM ON (is saying that we want to create a new database snapshot called backrecTestDB_snapshot_12AM. This is also the name of the snapshot when viewed within SSMS. The presence of the ON keyword means that it is based on an existing file. In this case, the NAME = attribute holds the logical name of the database file as found in your Database Properties window, as shown in Figure 8-16. You can find this information by right-clicking your database name, choosing Properties, and then clicking the Files menu option on the left to open the Files tab.

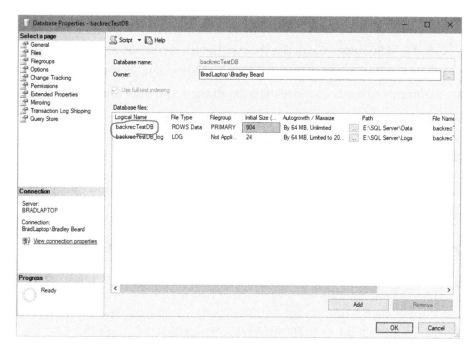

Figure 8-16. *Logical Name location*

The line FILENAME = 'E:\SQL Server\Data\backrecTestDB_data_12AM' lets us declare the name of the file to be saved in the file system. Finally, the line) AS SNAPSHOT OF backrecTestDB; lets us specifically define that we want to create a snapshot, and not a "regular" database. Copy Listing 8-5 into a New Query window and press F5 to run the script, after you have updated your database name for what I have. Next, switch over to Object Explorer and press the Refresh button in the toolbar and expand the Database Snapshots option underneath Databases. If the script in Listing 8-5 runs correctly, and the database snapshot was created, you will see what is shown in Figure 8-17.

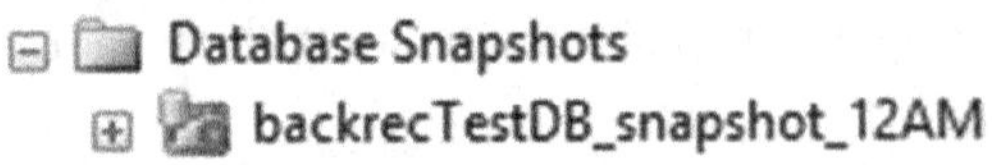

```
⊟ 📁 Database Snapshots
   ⊞ 📊 backrecTestDB_snapshot_12AM
```

Figure 8-17. *Database snapshot created successfully*

Good job! So now we can see that we have a snapshot, and if you were to expand the backrecTestDB_snapshot_12AM option, you would see the exact contents of the backrecTestDB database at the time that the snapshot was taken.

Querying a Database Snapshot

You would query a database snapshot the same way you would query the source database. Listing 8-6 shows both syntaxes.

Listing 8-6. Querying Source Databases and Snapshots

```
SELECT count(*) as cnt FROM [backrecTestDB_snapshot_12AM].dbo.
users2

SELECT count(*) as cnt FROM [backrecTestDB].dbo.users2
```

Once we run that, we see that we are at 10,000 rows in each table. This is to be expected, and is good because it shows that our data is consistent so far. What we want to do now is delete some data out of the source database and compare the two row counts again. The query I used is in Listing 8-7.

Listing 8-7. DELETE Snippet

```
DELETE FROM [backrecTestDB].dbo.users2 WHERE fname = 'Bradley'
```

Executing this code deletes 1000 rows out of the users2 table in the backrecTestDB database.

If we execute the code shown in Listing 8-6, we see there are 10,000 rows in the snapshot, and 9000 rows in the source database.

If we were to take another snapshot at this point, and then delete another set of data from the users2 table or make any other arbitrary change, then we would have three separate and distinct sets of data that we could restore from.

Using this example, you can see why I mentioned earlier about using snapshots as sources for reporting. Utilizing the data as a frozen point in time can open up a lot of possibilities within reporting.

Restoring a Database Snapshot

Now that we can see that I have two different databases with two sets of data that are not exactly the same, we can begin the process of restoring the snapshot on top of the source database, essentially undoing any operations done since the snapshot was taken.

In order to restore the database snapshot, we have to execute a RESTORE DATABASE command similar to what is shown in Listing 8-8.

Listing 8-8. RESTORE DATABASE Syntax

```
RESTORE DATABASE backrecTestDB
FROM DATABASE_SNAPSHOT = 'backrecTestDB_snapshot_12AM'
```

Before we run this, let's go over a couple of caveats about this operation.

- The code will run as long as there are no open connections to the database instance. If there are open connections, run the following code to close the connections before running the code in Listing 8-8:

```
ALTER DATABASE backrecTestDB
SET SINGLE_USER WITH
ROLLBACK IMMEDIATE
```

- We have to know that what we are restoring is the correct version of the data. Yes, that is why we created the naming convention, but it takes just a minute to query the snapshot and ensure that the data we need is definitely there. Unless, of course, you only have a single snapshot and you just made it specifically to restore from.

- When you have verified that the data is correct, then you must drop any other snapshots of the source database. The restore operation will not continue unless there is only a single snapshot.

- We cannot do point-in-time restores with snapshots. You get what is in the database, and that's it. For this reason, you must ensure that you are restoring the correct version of the data to be restored.

Go ahead and execute the code in Listing 8-8, and then immediately execute the code in Listing 8-6. Look at that; we are back to 10000 rows in the users2 database because we successfully restored the database snapshot.

Viewing Backup and Restore History

Ever wanted to see what is happening under the covers with your backup and restore operations? Poring through database tables can be monotonous, trust me. Luckily, SQL Server has quite a few reports built in, and one specifically that can help you with viewing backup and restore events is called Backup and Restore Events; how convenient! This report can be extremely useful in pinpointing any errors that may happen during backup and restore operations.

To run this report, right-click your database name (backrecTestDB, for me) and hover over Reports, then hover over Standard Reports, and select Backup and Restore Events. Figure 8-18 shows what the initial report screen looks like.

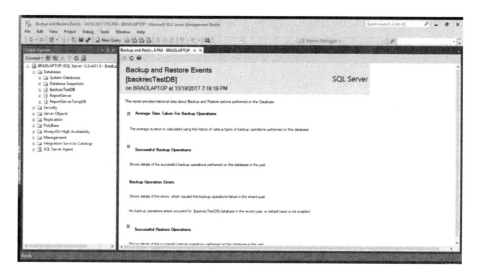

Figure 8-18. *Backup and Restore Events report*

There are four main headings in this report. They are as follows:

- Average Time Taken for Backup Operations

  - The average duration is calculated using the history of various types of backup operations performed on this database.

- Successful Backup Operations

  - Shows details of the successful backup operations performed on this database in the past.

- Backup Operation Errors

  - Shows details of the errors which caused the backup operations failure in the past.

- Successful Restore Operations

  - Shows details of the successful restore operations performed on this database in the past.

This report is very easy to navigate. All you need to do is click the little plus sign to expand the table. Inside, you will see that the table is sorted with the newest records on top.

Summary

This chapter saw us finally wrapping up the restore operations and learning about the different options of restoring data that are vital to the backup and restore operations.

We learned about restoring pages and the value of `msdb..suspect_pages` to find out about suspected corruption of the pages in the database.

We went over restoring from a database snapshot and all that entails.

And finally, we learned about viewing the history of the backup and restore history.

This chapter concludes this section on the restore aspect of the backup and restore operation. In the next section, we will start getting everything put together into a single separate backup and Restore plan.

PART III

Complete Solutions

CHAPTER 9

Full Backup and Restore Solutions

In the "real world," there is a definite business need to have reliable backups available at a moment's notice. The eventuality of data corruption is almost a guarantee, so the seasoned DBA must know that their database can be restored quickly and correctly. The availability and reliability of the backup are of utmost importance, whether backups are stored in a remote location or they are stored local to the database server. We often deal with service-level agreements, or SLAs, in our backup and recovery practices. This sort of document deals with a wide range of specifics, such as how often the backups are to be run, the conditions for restoring data, and how to restore the data. You may work in a place that doesn't deal with these, and that is fine also. For instance, if you are providing database storage as a service as part of a web hosting package, then you will more than likely be bound with an SLA which describes the specifics of the availability of that system. Whether or not you are bound by an SLA in your daily responsibilities as a DBA, the one thing that will not change is your responsibility to the well-being of the database and the data it houses. I have tried to get one message across in every book I have written so far, and this book is no different: there is no greater responsibility we have as DBAs than the protection of our data.

© Bradley Beard 2018
B. Beard, *Beginning Backup and Restore for SQL Server*,
https://doi.org/10.1007/978-1-4842-3456-3_9

In my personal experience, I can think of a grand total of one DBA that I know that has a complete backup scenario completely in T-SQL. This person's justification was that SQL could be run from outside of SSMS, so having it available outside of SSMS was ideal. While a part of me agrees with this, another part of me says that we should be leveraging the tools we have at our disposal, including (and especially) ones that we can use automate tasks such as backups. To me, it makes sense to have the bulk of the work done by SSMS, but still have the T-SQL available for the code hounds like my DBA friend in case we need to back up or restore the database and SSMS is not available to us for some reason. For this reason, we are going to focus this chapter on creating a maintenance plan for a full backup in SQL Server Management Studio, and then working up the corresponding T-SQL, in case we need it. Understand that this is not to say that T-SQL does not have its place as the main scripting tool for the seasoned or beginning DBA; to suggest otherwise makes no sense, since T-SQL is the underlying language that DBAs use to communicate with the database. There are many T-SQL solutions available on a simple Google search, and the one worth really mentioning is Ola Hallengren's backup script solution, located at `https://ola.hallengren.com/`.

Up until now, we have concentrated on the differences between backups and restores and kept them separated in our minds through the different chapters. We need to start to join those disparate concepts together now into a cohesive unit, and the best way that I can think of to do that is by creating two separate maintenance plans, one for backups and one for restores, to manage the different parts of the plan. The obvious implication of having separate maintenance plans is that there will be a different schedule in place for each backup portion.

For this chapter, we will go through how to create a maintenance plan for full backups. Now, clearly, we don't want to have the restore sequence as part of the backup scenario. The reason for this is because all we would be doing is running a full database backup, and then restoring that backup right on top of the database that we just backed up.

Listing 9-1 shows what we will build in this chapter.

Listing 9-1. To-Do List

- Full backup maintenance plan in SSMS

  - Based on our previous schedule, one full backup every 24 hours

  - Backups must be on a separate physical disk than the installation of SQL Server

- Full restore maintenance plan in SSMS

  - Not scheduled, but available to SSMS as an SQL Server Integration Services (SSIS) package

- Full backup maintenance plan in T-SQL

  - Not scheduled and can be run from `sqlcmd` when necessary

- Full restore maintenance plan in T-SQL

  - Not scheduled and can be run from `sqlcmd` when necessary

That seems like a pretty good start for this chapter. In the two chapters following this one, we will essentially build the same thing for our differential and transaction log backups.

Full Backup Plan in SSMS

Once we start up SSMS, with the focus on Object Explorer, we need to expand Management, and then expand Maintenance Plans. If we had any maintenance plans, they would be in this area. They would also be in the Jobs menu of SQL Server Agent as individual jobs, but we will take a look at that area once we create the maintenance plan.

Right-click Maintenance Plans and select New Maintenance Plan. When you see the New Maintenance Plan window shown in Figure 9-1, give it a name of Backup Plan and press OK.

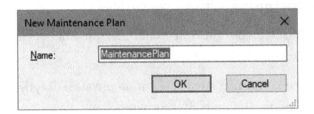

Figure 9-1. *New Maintenance Plan window*

Once you give it a name, a window titled Backup Plan [Design] is opened in the main stage area. Figure 9-2 shows the default values for this window.

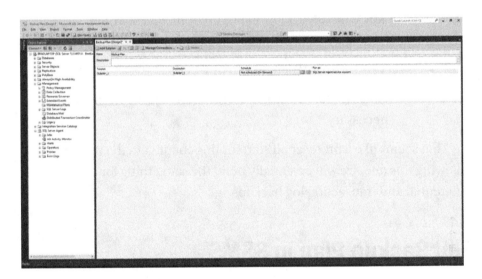

Figure 9-2. *Backup Plan [Design] window*

Next, we need to open up our Toolbox by clicking the Toolbox hovering menu located to the left of Object Explorer against the side of the interface. Alternately, you can press Ctrl+Alt+X anywhere within the SQL Server Management Studio screen and the menu will appear on the left as an overlay on top of Object Explorer. To hide the Toolbar, just click the Toolbar hovering menu again and it will disappear, leaving Object Explorer in view.

The toolbox has quite a few items that I explored at great length in my first book, *Practical Maintenance Plans in SQL Server* (www.apress.com/us/book/9781484218945). We can see from a cursory glance at Figure 9-3 that the option we want is right there on top; we want the Back Up Database Task.

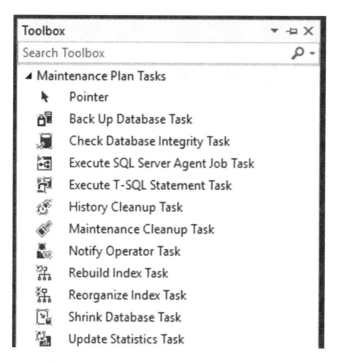

Figure 9-3. *Toolbox*

Click and drag the Back Up Database Task from the Toolbox to the gray area of the main stage. Figure 9-4 shows approximately where the task should end up in the stage, but just anywhere inside of the stage is fine. The stage area acts as the logical container for the pieces of the maintenance plan, and the order they are in doesn't matter in the slightest. The only thing that can interconnect these pieces is the precedence constraints that we could put on each successive item, so that we can chain events together and make the maintenance plan a bit more procedural than just a scheduled lump of tasks.

Once you drag the Back Up Database Task onto the stage, you will see it appear as shown in Figure 9-4. Note that the red X signifies that this item needs to be configured.

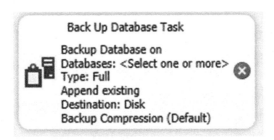

Figure 9-4. Back Up Database Task

If you were to mouse over the red X, you would see the message "No connection manager is specified." Double-click the task and the Back Up Database Task window appears, as shown in Figure 9-5.

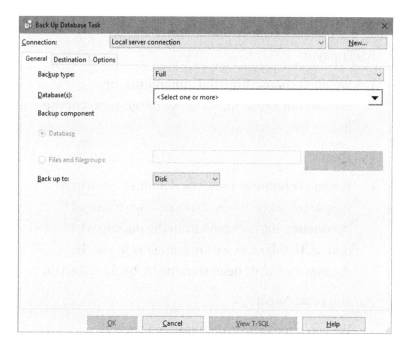

Figure 9-5. *Back Up Database Task window*

For those that are familiar with this area from previous versions of SQL Server, you will notice that this interface got a slight upgrade in this version of SQL Server Management Studio. It may even be different once SQL Server Management Studio is updated again, since SSMS is now a separate download from SQL Server and therefore subject to an update cycle outside of the service pack issuance by Microsoft.

Defining the Back Up Database Task Options

Note that we are on the General tab. This is where we are going to specify the items shown in Listing 9-2 in order to get this area prepared.

Listing 9-2. To-Do List

- Backup type

  - We must choose from full, differential, or transaction log. In this case, we are going to choose full.

- Databases

  - We must choose at least one database. Note that simple recovery model databases are removed if transaction log is chosen from the backup type option. In this case, we are going to choose the database we have been working in, backrecTestDB.

- Backup component

  - We can choose from database or files and filegroups. In this case, we are going to choose database. We could choose files and filegroups if we had multiple filegroups for our database, but I only set up the PRIMARY filegroup.

Note   If you have multiple filegroups in your scenario, then you can setup multiple full backup tasks to backup each filegroup in the order or schedule you desire.

- Back up to

  - We must choose from disk, tape, or URL. In this case, keep it set to disk.

Above the General tab, we can see the Connection drop-down menu. This defaults to "Local server connection" and it needs to stay there for this procedure.

Once you make the changes noted in Listing 9-2, your window should look similar to what is shown in Figure 9-6.

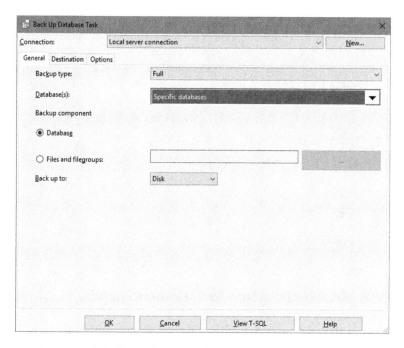

Figure 9-6. *Back Up Database Task, updated*

Note that the Databases area changes to the text "Specific databases" when a database is selected.

When you are ready, select the Destination tab to proceed. Figure 9-7 shows the default settings for this tab.

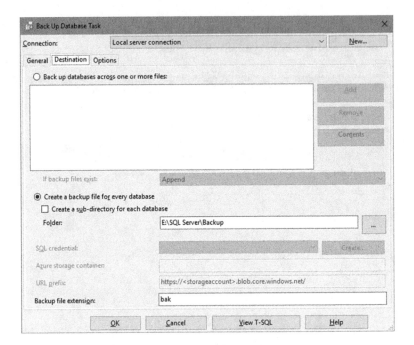

Figure 9-7. *Back Up Database Task, Destination tab*

This tab is slightly more complicated than the General tab. In here, we have the options detailed in Listing 9-3.

Listing 9-3. Destination Tab Options

- Back up databases across one or more files

  - This option exists in case we want to create multiple backup files of the same database. We can add as many different file names in this area as we would like, but note that there will be performance issues with too many entries.

- Create a backup file for every database

  - This is probably the most common option,
    since it lets us have a single backup file of every
    selected database. You can also select to create
    a subdirectory for each database, which is a very
    handy feature as well. The folder location is where
    the database backup will be placed, unless the
    subdirectory option is checked, in which case, the
    database name will become a folder name, and
    the backup will be placed inside that folder. We
    want to choose this option, and check the Create a
    subdirectory for each database check box as well.
    Leave the folder value as is, since the default value
    for backups is a unique date/time string.

Notice that there is another section under Listing 9-3 options that are
defined as shown in Listing 9-4. These options are only available if you
chose the URL option in the General tab shown in Figure 9-5. Otherwise,
they are disabled by default.

Listing 9-4. Azure Options

- SQL Credential

  - This is the SQL Credential account used to connect
    to the Azure database.

- Azure storage container

  - An Azure storage container is like a block of storage
    that you can use for just about anything you want.
    In this instance, we are specifically referring to a
    database backup, but it isn't backing up directly to
    an Azure instance; instead, it is just backing up the
    file to cloud-based storage.

- URL prefix

  - The URL prefix is unique to each account. You get
    a storage account name from Microsoft when you
    sign up for Azure, and the storage account name
    will be the prefix in the URL.

After these options, the last item is Backup file extension, which is
defaulted to bak. This can be changed to whatever extension you desire,
but I would leave this alone and accept the default value. Figure 9-8 shows
the updated values for the Destination tab.

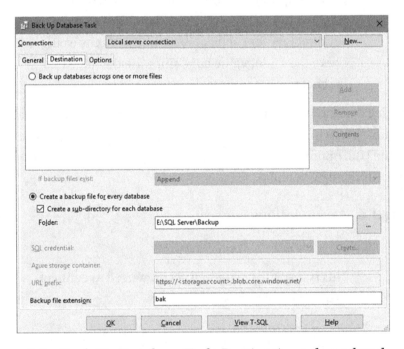

Figure 9-8. *Back Up Database Task, Destination tab, updated*

When you are ready to move on, click the Options tab and you will see
the default values shown in Figure 9-9.

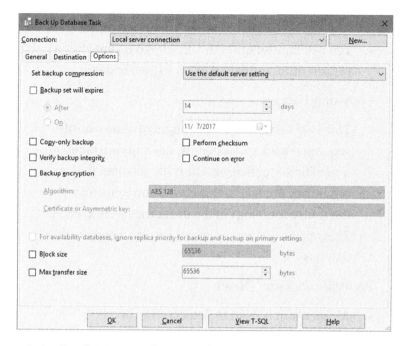

Figure 9-9. *Back Up Database Task, Options tab*

By default, these options are all okay. However, let's step through them in Listing 9-5 so that we understand what we are looking at.

Listing 9-5. Options Tab... Options?

- Set backup compression

    - Allows you to set the compression type for the backup. The three options are as follows:

    - Use the default server setting

    - Compress backup

    - Do not compress backup

- Backup set will expire

  - You can choose to set the backup to expire after a certain number of days or on a specific date.

- Copy-only backup

  - This backup type can be thought of as an out-of-sequence backup. Generally, backups are taken in a specific sequence, and must be restored in the order they are taken; this is why you must restore the transaction logs in the order they were created. This option allows you to only create a copy of the database.

- Perform checksum (New)

  - A checksum is used to detect errors or inconsistencies in data. In this context, a checksum is done on the newly generated backup file to ensure that it is consistent with what was believed to be produced.

- Verify backup integrity

  - This option is the same as running a `RESTORE VERIFYONLY` command on your backup file location. The simple syntax is `RESTORE VERIFYONLY FROM DISK = <backup file location and name>`. Its purpose is to verify the integrity of the newly generated backup file (that was redundant!).

- Continue on error (New)

  - Simply put, to ignore any errors and keep hammering away... unless a fatal error occurs, which would stop the program from executing.

- Backup encryption

  - In this area, you can choose the algorithm and certificate or asymmetric key for decryption. Be very careful with this area, because the same certificate or asymmetric key must be used if you ever want to restore the generated backup. If the certificate or key is lost, the backup cannot be restored successfully.

- For availability databases, ignore replica priority for backup and backup on primary settings

  - When dealing with AlwaysOn and Availability Groups, I always default to my good friend Peter Carter's excellent book *SQL Server AlwaysOn Revealed* (`www.apress.com/us/book/9781484217634`). This option allows us to tell the availability databases to back up the database instance using the primary settings for the database.

- Block size (New)

  - This option allows you to specify the physical block size in bytes, as opposed to allowing the SQL Server resource governor to handle the backup using the default options. Setting this to a lower value would have an adverse effect on backup operations, but smaller chunks of data would be written instead of large chunks.

- Max transfer size (New)

  - This option allows you to specify the largest unit of transfer in bytes to be used between SQL Server and the backup media.

The block size and max transfer size options sound very similar, don't you think? The difference between them is that the block size option allows you to say to SQL Server, "I know you usually take a certain number of bytes, but I want you to take a different number of bytes and put them in the backup location." The max transfer size option allows you to say to SQL Server, "When you move bytes to the backup location, I want that chunk to be a specific size. You can pack as many blocks into that transfer size that you want, but once you reach the limit I set, you need to make another trip." In other words, think of block size as the individual train car and the max transfer size as the entire train. Therefore, the max transfer size option is always larger than the block size option. For example, check the block size and max transfer size check boxes. Then choose 4096 in the block size drop-down menu. Next, type in an amount in the max transfer size area; I chose 512. Finally, press Tab to move out of the max transfer size area. Did you see the value change back to 65536? Next, click the up arrow on the max transfer size area, and it will change to 131072. Click the down arrow twice, and it will default to 65536, but it will not go lower.

Before we continue, make sure you uncheck the block size and max transfer size check boxes. Leaving them checked probably wouldn't cause a lot of headache, but I don't want to introduce anything into the mix that would possibly cause an error. The options I selected in here were Verify backup integrity and Perform checksum. Figure 9-10 shows the updated interface for the Options tab.

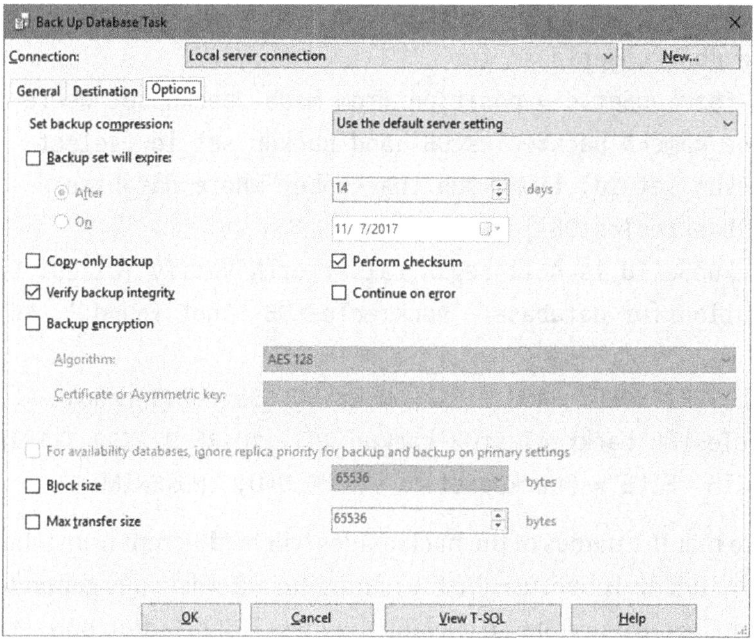

Figure 9-10. *Back Up Database Task, Options tab, updated*

That's all the options in this area that I needed to have for the full backup option. Before we move on, I want to look at the generated T-SQL from this plan, so click the View T-SQL button, and you will see something similar to what is shown in Listing 9-6.

Listing 9-6. Full Backup in T-SQL

```
EXECUTE master.dbo.xp_create_subdir N'E:\SQL Server\Backup\
backrecTestDB'
GO
BACKUP DATABASE [backrecTestDB] TO DISK = N'E:\SQL Server\
Backup\backrecTestDB\backrecTestDB_backup_2017_10_26_
223559_7118287.bak' WITH NOFORMAT, NOINIT,  NAME =
N'backrecTestDB_backup_2017_10_26_223559_7118287', SKIP,
REWIND, NOUNLOAD,  STATS = 10, CHECKSUM
```

213

```
GO
declare @backupSetId as int
select @backupSetId = position from msdb..backupset where
database_name=N'backrecTestDB' and backup_set_id=(select
max(backup_set_id) from msdb..backupset where database_
name=N'backrecTestDB')
if @backupSetId is null begin raiserror(N'Verify failed. Backup
information for database ''backrecTestDB'' not found.', 16, 1)
end
RESTORE VERIFYONLY FROM DISK = N'E:\SQL Server\Backup\
backrecTestDB\backrecTestDB_backup_2017_10_26_223559_7118287.
bak' WITH  FILE = @backupSetId,  NOUNLOAD,  NOREWIND
```

Note that the names of the backup files will be different from what is shown here. This is because the file names are automatically generated based on the current time, so clicking the View T-SQL button one second apart will generate two different file names. This listing should be used as a template to paste in the backup name that you want to backup AND what you want to verify after backup. Do not just save this script and expect it to run on your machine; I guarantee you that it will fail spectacularly.

When you are ready, click OK to continue. Notice that the red X goes away now, and we are left with what is shown in Figure 9-11.

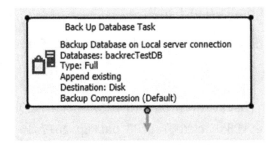

Figure 9-11. *Backup Plan [Design], updated*

Scheduling the Full Backup

Now that we have our plan set up, we need to set up a schedule. Typically, the schedule I employ at home and at work is almost the same; a full backup at midnight, a differential backup every six hours, and a transaction log backup every hour. There are some instances where I would even run the transaction log backups every half-hour, but this would introduce a lot more files to have to restore from, while cutting the maximum time for data loss in half.

Starting from where we left off, we can now see what is shown in Figure 9-12.

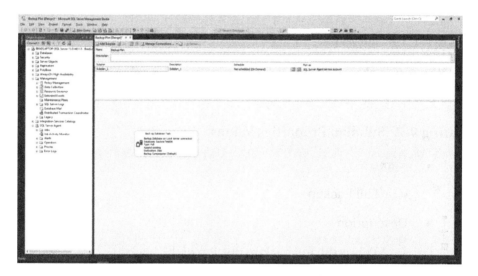

Figure 9-12. *Backup Plan [Design] stage*

Notice that we now have a subplan named Subplan_1 in the section above the stage. This is the plan for the full backup, but we need to give it a better name. Double-click the Subplan, Description, or Schedule column to open the Subplan Properties window shown in Figure 9-13.

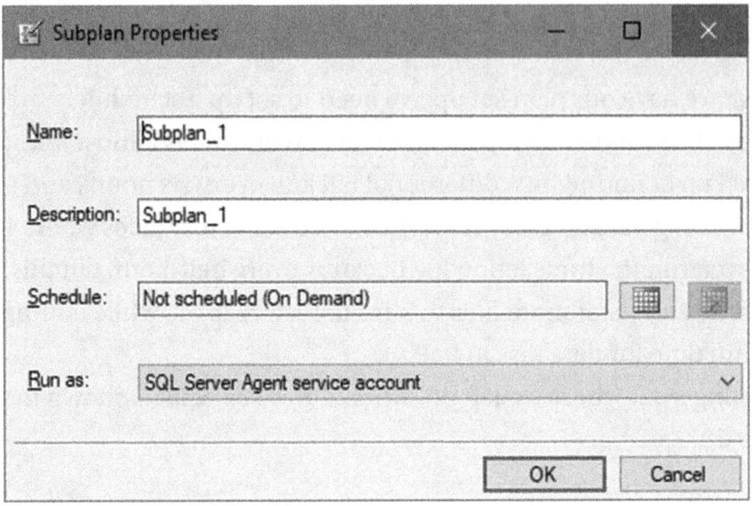

Figure 9-13. *Subplan Properties*

We want to change the default values to the values shown in Listing 9-7.

Listing 9-7. Subplan Properties Values

- Name
  - "Full Backup"
- Description
  - "This is the full backup portion of the backup maintenance plan"
- Schedule
  - We will set this up in a different area, so ignore this for now
- Run as
  - Keep this as the default

Once you have updated those values, click OK to close that window and you will be returned to the main stage. Figure 9-14 shows the updated values in the Subplan Properties window that you should see, and Figure 9-15 shows the updated stage at this point as well.

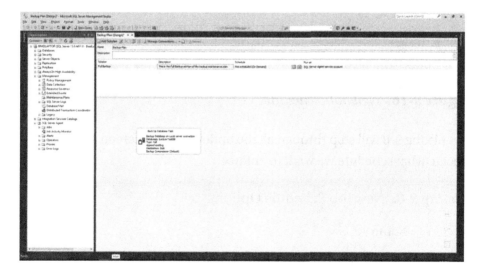

Figure 9-14. *Subplan Properties, updated*

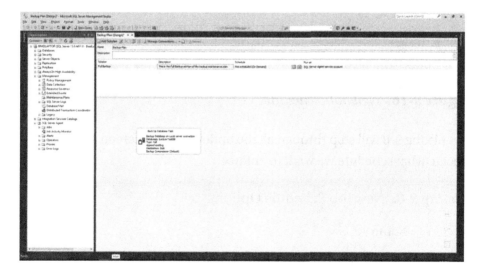

Figure 9-15. *Updated stage*

We can see in Figure 9-15 that our values have been updated in the Subplan row to the values we entered. For the schedule, we opted to wait until a bit later, so let's look at that now.

Click the calendar icon in the row next to the Schedule column. Figure 9-16 shows the initial interface for the New Job Schedule screen.

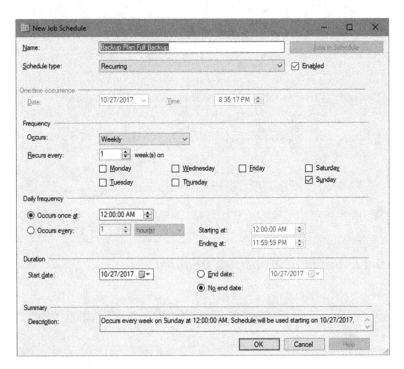

Figure 9-16. *New Job Schedule*

Listing 9-8 will step through all the options on this screen so we can decide what schedule we want to enforce.

Listing 9-8. New Job Schedule Options

- Name

    - The name of the scheduled job. The default value is fine here.

- Schedule type
    - Available options are
        - Start automatically when SQL Server Agent starts
        - Start whenever the CPUs become idle
        - Recurring
        - One time
- One-time occurrence
    - If the One time option is selected in the Schedule type drop-down menu, then this option is available. Otherwise, it is disabled.
- Frequency
    - Occurs
        - Available options are
            - Daily
            - Weekly
            - Monthly
    - Recurs every
        - If Daily is selected in the Occurs drop-down menu, then you can choose any number of days, up to 100.
        - If Weekly is selected in the Occurs drop-down menu, then you can choose a number of weeks, up to 100. Additionally, you can choose the day of the week that the plan is run on; the default value is Sunday, but any combination of days of the week can be selected.

- If Monthly is selected in the Occurs drop-down menu, then you can choose to run the plan on day <number> of every <number> month(s); for example, you can choose the fourth day of every second month, or the first day of every month. You can also choose to run the plan on the <number> <day of the week> of every <number> month(s); for example, the second Tuesday of every third month.

- Daily frequency

  - Occurs once at

    - A set time to run the schedule

  - Occurs every

    - Run the scheduled task every <number> hour(s), starting at the starting time and ending at the ending time selected. If nothing is selected, the default values are retained.

- Duration

  - How long to run the scheduled task for; not the execution time of the task, meaning the time that it takes a task to run a single backup operation, but the availability of the task before it "expires."

- Summary

  - This is a plain-English summary of the selected options.

The interface in Figure 9-17 shows the updated values for the New Job Schedule screen. Note that the Enabled check box is checked; this wouldn't go very far if that weren't checked.

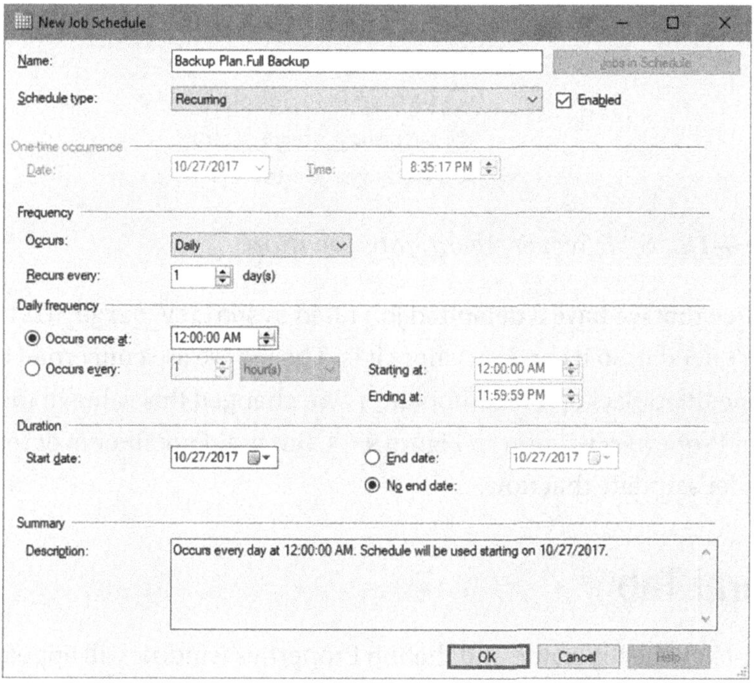

Figure 9-17. *New Job Schedule, updated*

When you get your schedule set how you would like, press OK to return to the stage and notice that the Schedule column is updated with the Summary text from the New Job Schedule interface.

Updating the SQL Server Agent Job

Now that we have the maintenance plan set up, we could leave it alone and have it run normally. However, the SQL Server Agent job needs to be updated. Why? Because for some reason, the job doesn't inherit all of the values from the maintenance plan, and we have to go in and backfill the job values. This will hopefully change in future versions of SSMS.

Expand the SQL Server Agent menu from Object Explorer, and then expand Jobs. Figure 9-18 shows the location of this menu item.

Figure 9-18. *SQL Server Agent, Jobs location*

Notice that we have a defaulted job titled `syspolicy_purge_history`. We don't need it, so it can stay where it is. The job we are concerned about is the one titled Backup Plan.Subplan_1. We changed this value in the Subplan Properties window in Figure 9-14, but it did not filter over to this area, so let's update that now.

General Tab

Double-click the job name and the Job Properties window will appear as shown in Figure 9-19. The purpose of this tab is to give the top-level, or "General," settings for the job. Don't think that this area is not important though, because a lot can go wrong if it is not filled out correctly. For example, the Enabled check box needs to stay checked, and the owner needs to stay as an account with permission to the database, or the database owner from the Properties window of the database.

Note   Right-click the database name and select Properties. From here, you can view the owner of the database. This is not to be confused with the dbo role.

In my experience, those two values need to match. If they don't, as I said, then this value needs to be of a user with access to the database.

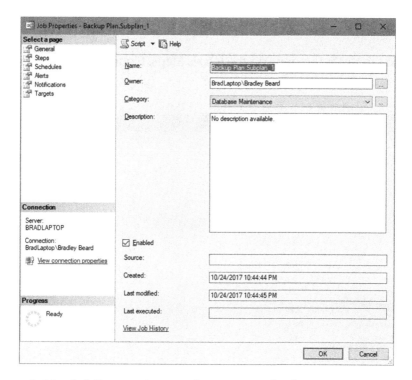

Figure 9-19. *Job Properties window, General tab*

As you can see, a few of the options we set in the previous section didn't transfer to this job, such as the name and the description. Update the Name field to say Full Backup and enter a short description to complete the items on the General tab. Notice that the Category option can be pulled down and different options can be selected. The purpose of this is to allow you to segregate different jobs into different categories, and then use those different categories for log checking or reporting purposes. It defaults to Database Maintenance though, so it's best to keep it there.

When you are satisfied with your settings in this area, click the Steps tab.

Steps Tab

The next tab (from the pane on the left) is Steps. Figure 9-20 shows the default settings in this page.

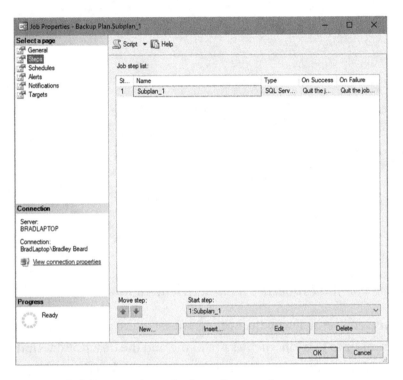

Figure 9-20. *Job Properties window, Steps tab*

If we had multiple steps in this job, they would be shown here. Alternately, we could add some jobs in here that are outside of the maintenance plan creation we did earlier. We don't want to do that right now, but it is an option to think about for your own plans, if necessary.

Notice again that the name is different? So, again, we need to double-click that row and update those values. Figure 9-21 shows the initial values for the Job Step Properties – Subplan_1 window.

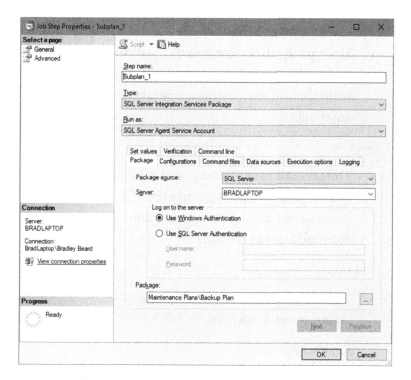

Figure 9-21. *Job Step Properties – Subplan_1, General tab*

Job Step Properties - Subplan_1 (General Tab)

Be very careful in this area. You could really do some damage in here to both this job and your database. This area essentially lets you set up the properties and values for the SSIS package that will be created as a result of creating this job.

Listing 9-9 shows the available options in this tab.

Listing 9-9. Job Step Properties - Subplan_1 Options

- Step name

  - The name of the step.

- Type

    - The type of job being created. There are quite a few options in here that have absolutely nothing to do with what we are creating, so be sure to not change anything.

- Run as

    - The account to use to execute the package. The default value is always going to be SQL Server Agent because this account has permission to execute SSIS packages by default.

- Package

    - This subtab lets you define basic package characteristics, such as

        - Package source

            - Where the package will be created: SQL Server, File System, SSIS Package Store, or SSIS Catalog.

        - Server

            - The target server for the deployment of the SSIS package.

        - Log on to the server

            - Login information for manual execution of the package.

        - Package

            - The default location for saving the package. This value is determined by the value selected in the Package source drop-down menu. For example, you cannot specify a Windows folder location and the SQL Server option, because the SQL Server option expects the package to reside within the SQL Server logical tree shown as Maintenance Plans\Backup Plan.

- Configurations

  - If there are any configuration files, they would be added in this area.

- Command files

  - If there are any command files, they would be added in this area.

- Data sources

  - If a data source needs to be added that is separate and distinct from the current data source, then it can be added here.

- Execution options

  - Depending on the option selected, these options can be available before or during package execution. The available options are

    - Fail the package on validation warnings [DURING]: This will fire when the package is executing in order to fail the package on any warnings.

- Validate package without executing [BEFORE]: The package will not execute, and only be validated.

- Override MaxConcurrentExecutables property [BEFORE]: This option is to make sure that too many executables aren't jockeying for CPU time.

- Enable package checkpoints [DURING]: If enabled, the package will send status updates at every step.

- Use 32-bit runtime [BEFORE]: This option defines whether or not to execute this package in a 32-bit runtime or the default 64-bit runtime.

- Logging

  - A fantastic option that a lot of people don't even know about it the built-in logging available in this area. SSIS has a default log provider, and those available options are SSIS log provider for

    - SSIS log provider for text files

    - SSIS log provider for SQL Server

    - SSIS log provider for Windows event log

    - SSIS log provider for SQL server profiler

    - SSIS log provider for XML files

- Set values

  - If you have any values that you want to set for the package, you can add them here.

- Verification

    - This is sort of a step beyond the options in the
      preceding execution options. This area is more for
      the verification of the package from a security point
      of view. Available options in here are

        - Execute only signed packages

        - Verify package build

        - Verify package ID

        - Verify version ID

- Command line

    - Any command-line options can be added here,
      and they will be added in the context of the user
      executing the package. Make absolutely sure that
      if you change this area, the Run as account has
      permission to execute the specified commands in
      this area.

The only thing you want to update here is the Step name, if required.
All of the other settings are defaulted to where we need them to be. When
you have updated the Step name value, click the Advanced tab.

Job Step Properties - Subplan_1 (Advanced Tab)

The Advanced tab holds the options for the reporting and logging actions.
Figure 9-22 shows the default values in this area, which are mostly correct
for what we need.

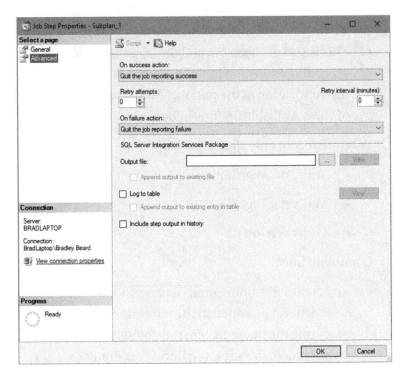

Figure 9-22. Job Step Properties – Subplan_1, Advanced tab

Notice that the default options are exactly what you would expect; when the package executes successfully, it quits the job reporting a success. If it fails, it quits the job reporting a failure. Let's take a closer look at these options and what they really mean. Listing 9-10 breaks down these options.

Listing 9-10. Advanced Tab Options

- On success action

    - When the step completes successfully, what should the package do? Available options here are

        - Go to the next step

            - If there is another step in this package, go do that next step.

- Quit the job reporting success

  - Default.

- Quit the job reporting failure

  - It's sort of a matter of miscommunication to report a failure for a successfully executed job, so the only thing I can think that this option would be for would be if the package execution was intended to return a failure.

- Retry attempts

  - The number of retry attempts that this package is allowed.

- Retry interval (minutes)

  - The amount of time to wait in between package retries.

- On failure action

  - Same options as previously, except the logic for the Quit the job reporting success option is reversed.

- Output file

  - When the SSIS package is executed, then an output log file is generated. It can be entered here for later review.

- Log to table

  - Checking this option allows you to log the results of the package execution to the sysjobstepslogs table in the msdb database.

- Include step output in history

  - This option allows for greater accuracy in the SQL
    Server Agent logs of package execution.

Notice I said that these settings were only mostly correct. We want to check the Log to table and Include step output in history check boxes, and that's the only change we want to make here. Figure 9-23 shows the updated values for this screen, so update your screen and, when you're ready, click the OK button to close this window, save the settings, and return to the Job Properties window.

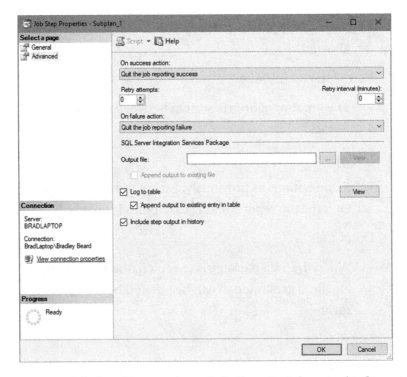

Figure 9-23. *Job Step Properties – Subplan_1, Advanced tab, updated*

Once we get back to the Job Properties window, we can see that the name of the job has been updated. Note that the Start step value is shown as Subplan_1 and not Full Backup. The reason for this is because the job hasn't been saved yet, although the values are shown in this interface.

Once we click OK on this screen, these values will be updated. We aren't going to do that yet though, so go ahead and click the Schedules tab on the left.

Schedules Tab

When you click the Schedules tab, you should see an empty interface; there should not be a schedule in this area. This is perfect, because we are scheduling this through the maintenance plan and not the SSIS package. Click the Alerts tab to continue.

Alerts Tab

We don't have any alerts set up for this job, but if you would like to have an alert, you can set it up here. An alert in this context means that SQL Server will alert you when an error or event occurs. SQL Server can also generate a response from the database, e-mail or page any Operators, and even send a NET SEND message. We aren't going to do anything to this area, because we are going to handle the notifications for this job in the next tab, coincidentally titled Notifications. Click the Notifications tab to continue.

Notifications Tab

The initial interface for this screen is shown in Figure 9-24. Note that the only option selected here is Write to the Windows Application event log. That is good, but we need more notification than just an entry in a log somewhere that we have to go and search for, and then try and figure out the exact cause of the error. Instead, we can use this area to set up real-time notifications for any failures of this job.

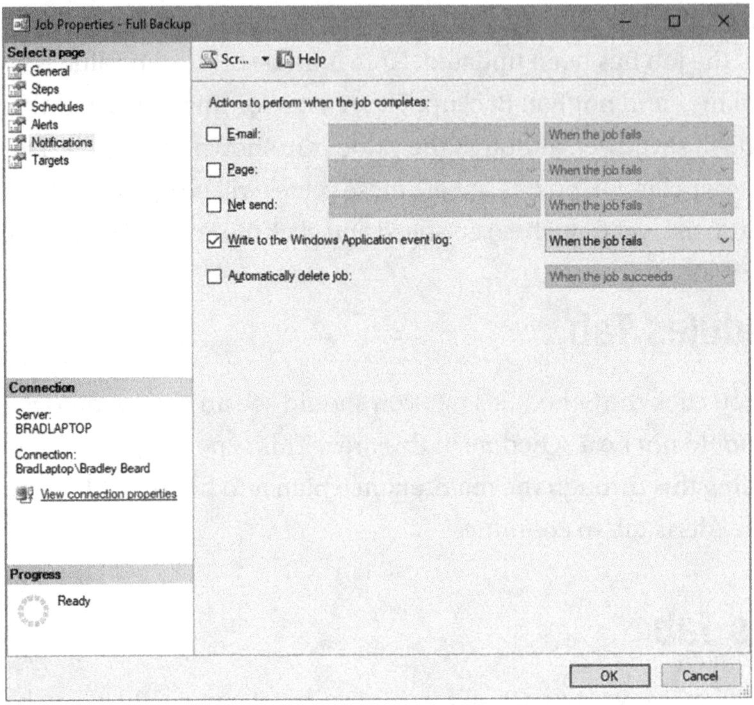

Figure 9-24. *Job Step Properties – Subplan_1, Notifications tab*

Listing 9-11 shows the various options and values in this area. To use the E-mail, Page, and Net send options, you must already have an Operator established. I will go into how to set up an Operator in the next section, since we will be using this functionality.

Listing 9-11. Notifications Options

- E-mail

  - This is probably the most used option, since e-mail is so prevalent. Just select the Operator with a verified e-mail, and then select the condition from the drop-down menu.

- Page

    - For those datacenters that still use pagers, this is a great way to keep in contact. Alternatively, you can think of texting someone as the functional equivalent of paging someone if they do not have a pager.

- Net send

    - If your PC and the database server are on the same network and your PC has a direct connection to the database server, then you can use Net send to send a message directly to your PC from the database server. This message appears as a modal dialog box on your PC.

- Write to the Windows Application event log

    - The only selected option by default in this area. Not a bad idea to keep this checked.

- Automatically delete job

    - As with before, I can't imagine an instance when I would want to delete a job after it finishes, mainly because the history for the job is either deleted or obfuscated, and there goes any forensic information we may need for the job.

For each of these options, the drop-down menu on the right has the following three options:

- When the job succeeds

    - The entire job must be a success.

- When the job fails

  - The entire job must be a failure.

- When the job completes

  - The entire job simply must complete, whether a success or failure.

This section is complete, so click the OK button to save changes and return to the stage once again. Notice that the job name is now updated to Full Backup in the Jobs submenu of the SQL Server Agent menu in Object Explorer. We will return to this Notifications tab after we finish setting up an Operator.

Setting Up an Operator

In my first book, *Practical Maintenance Plans in SQL Server*, I detailed how to set up a new Operator using the Alerts tab. There is a method to add a new Operator in that section, but I wanted to devote this section to using the Operators submenu from the SQL Server Agent menu in Object Explorer.

An Operator in this context is a person responsible for receiving information about the state of the database at the time that events occur. They may not necessarily be the person that can mitigate the circumstance, but they are a person that can trigger an action to encourage the change. For example, an executive might want to be notified when a backup fails for their own edification, but I seriously doubt that this executive will be able to fix the issue.

At this point, your SQL Server Agent menu should appear as shown in Figure 9-25, specifically in regards to the updated job name.

☐ 🔖 SQL Server Agent
    ☐ 📁 Jobs
        📇 Full Backup
        📇 syspolicy_purge_history
      🗂 Job Activity Monitor
    ⊞ 📁 Alerts
    ⊞ 📁 Operators
    ⊞ 📁 Proxies
    ⊞ 📁 Error Logs

Figure 9-25. *SQL Server Agent menu*

Right-click Operators and choose New Operator… to continue. The initial interface is shown in Figure 9-26.

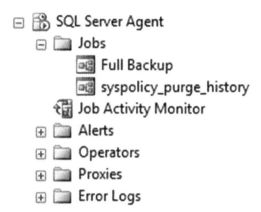

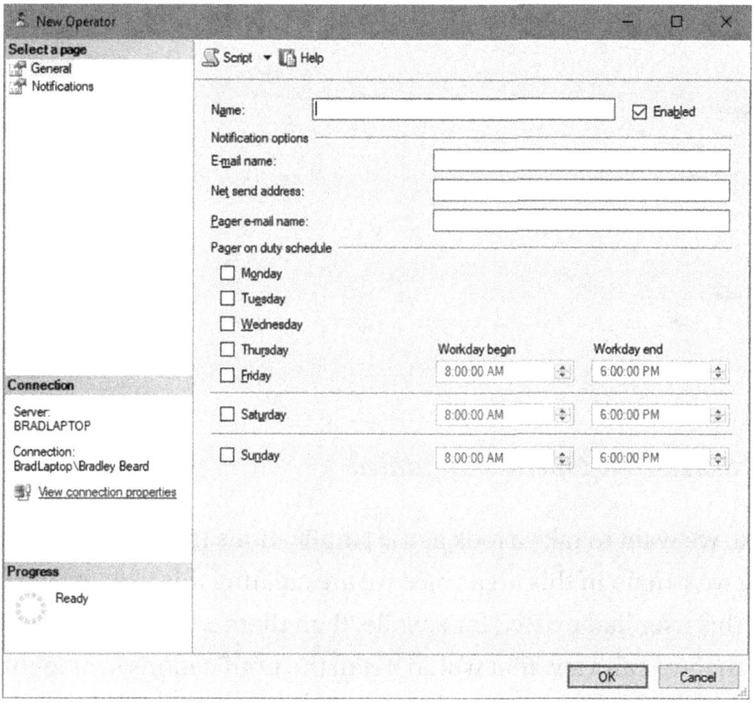

Figure 9-26. *New Operator*

We are going to enter the actual name of the person that will be receiving the notifications in the Name field, and their e-mail in the E-mail name field. If you have a NET SEND address, you can enter it here. Same thing with the pager information; if you have this info, enter it here. If you don't have this info or don't need to use it, then you can just leave it blank.

Once you have entered this information, you should have an interface very similar to what is shown in Figure 9-27.

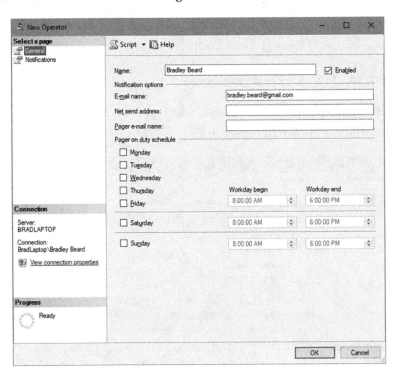

Figure 9-27. *New Operator, updated*

Next, we want to take a look at the Notifications tab, although there is nothing we can do in this area since we are creating this user for the first time. If this user had existed for a while, then there would be information in here that we can view that would detail the notifications sent to this user. This would be advantageous if there were an instance when a user disputed the receipt of a notification, for instance.

Go ahead and click the OK button to proceed with creating this Operator. Notice that our Operators submenu now has the entry of the username we just created. This means that this user is now available to be assigned as an Operator within the job, so double-click Full Backup Job again and click the Notifications tab. This will bring up the window shown in Figure 9-24, except we can now add our Operator. Figure 9-28 shows this option available in the Notifications tab of the Job Properties window.

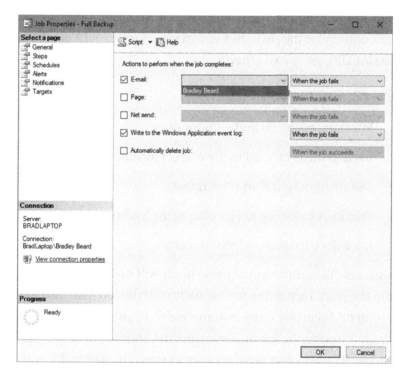

Figure 9-28. *Operator available*

I chose my new Operator, kept the event drop-down menu set to When the job fails, and then clicked OK. This added my Operator user to the Notifications tab, which means that I will be receiving e-mails if this job fails.

That's all for setting up the maintenance plan. We have defined the actual parameters of the task, and set up and enabled an Operator to receive notifications of failure. Next, we need to test this plan to make sure that it is executing properly.

Testing the Full Backup Plan

In order to properly determine if our plan is working correctly, we need to define exit criteria for the plan. In this instance, Listing 9-12 details what we will be looking for as exit criteria.

Listing 9-12. Exit Criteria

- Job starts correctly and without error

- Backup file is created in the correct location

- Notification sent if an error occurs

- Windows event log keeps a log of the backup operation

- Job exits correctly and without error

The successful completion of these items will determine the overall success of the plan. I am going to manually start the job instead of waiting until midnight for it run automatically. I can start the job at any time by right-clicking the job and selecting the Start Job at Step... option. Alternatively, if I wanted to run the entire maintenance plan, I could right-click the maintenance plan name and select the Execute option. I just want to check the job first, so right-click the job and execute it as noted previously. It runs for a few seconds, and then we can see that a new directory was created in E:\SQL Server\Backup named backrecTestDB, and a new backup file was placed in the directory. We also see a success message in a dialog window shown in Figure 9-29.

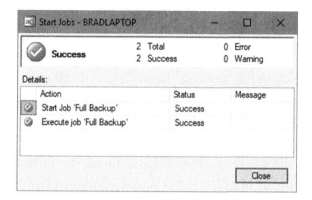

Figure 9-29. *Success message*

If we open up the Windows event log and go to the Application log, we will see what is shown in Figure 9-30, which is confirmation that Windows sees our backup action as a successful task.

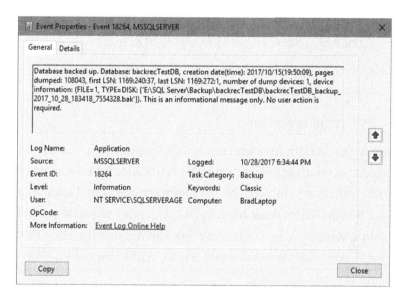

Figure 9-30. *Windows Application event log*

The only thing we didn't test at this point is the Notifications option, which did not fire because it did not fail.

Full Restore Plan in SSMS

This section will detail how to get a solid Restore plan from available backup files. The good thing about this section is that it is dependent solely upon there being a backup set of data to restore; if there is not a backup to restore from, then we cannot restore any data.

In SSMS, there is not a restore database task that we can run. Instead, we need to use the T-SQL commands for restoring the database, and wrap that command inside of a SQL Server Agent job that we can execute on demand. The basic structure for how we plan to implement this is simple, as shown in Listing 9-13.

Listing 9-13. Structure for Restoring Data

- Use known-good RESTORE DATABASE command from Chapter 5 as basis for T-SQL syntax

- Create SQL Server Agent job with T-SQL type

- Create a copy of the current full backup and rename it backrecTestDB.bak

- Restore data normally

I want to pause right here and make a quick point: the reason that we are copying and renaming our backup file is because I do not want to break the restore chain that is in place by the maintenance plan. I want to use the same data, but the script must have a static file name to reference in the restore script, which is why I chose to copy and rename the file. I'm sure there are different ways to handle this aspect, and if you have a different way of handling this, excellent!

T-SQL Restore Command

Referencing back to Chapter 5, the command that we used to restore the data was

```
RESTORE DATABASE backrecTestDB
FROM DISK = 'E:\SQL Server\Backup\backrecTestDB\backrecTestDB.bak'
WITH REPLACE
GO
```

We will use this same command in our restore job, so make a note of the FROM DISK location because we will need to use that location when we rename our file in this section.

SQL Server Agent Restore Job

To start this section off, we need to create a SQL Server Agent job without first creating a maintenance plan. Expand SQL Server Agent and right-click Jobs, then select New Job... to continue. The New Job window opens as shown in Figure 9-31; note that it is slightly different from the window we saw earlier that had some of the information referenced from the maintenance plan.

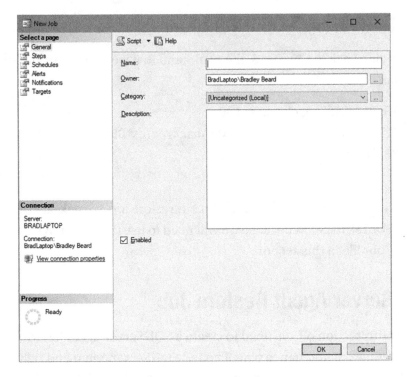

Figure 9-31. *New Job window, General tab*

It's a literal blank slate for us to create whatever we want. On this screen, we want to update the following values in Listing 9-14.

Listing 9-14. New Job Values

- Name
  - Update to full restore
- Owner
  - This should either be the sa (main admin) account in SQL Server, or a custom server agent service account, not a regular user account
- Category
  - Change this to database maintenance

- Description

    - Enter something like "This is the full restore portion of the full Restore plan"

Also, we want to make sure that the Enabled check box stays checked. Next, we want to select the Steps tab on the left. A blank window opens as shown in Figure 9-32.

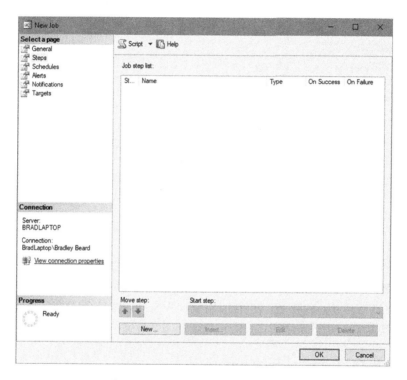

Figure 9-32. *New Job window, Steps tab*

For this page, we are going to click the New... button on the bottom of the screen and see the New Job Step screen shown in Figure 9-33.

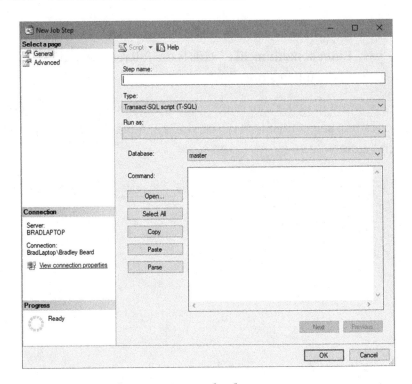

Figure 9-33. *New Job Step, General tab*

Again, this is a new interface for us. We may be used to seeing this screen with information prepopulated from a maintenance plan, but this is actually very easy. Next, we need to update the values shown in Listing 9-15.

Listing 9-15. General Tab Options

- Step name

  - Full Restore T-SQL Command

- Type

  - Transact-SQL script (T-SQL)

- Run as

    - (This value cannot be updated yet)

- Database

    - Master

- Command

    - Paste the T-SQL script from the T-SQL Restore Command section.

Notice that we can't update the Run as: value yet. This is okay for now, since we have to save these values and then come back to this screen again. You should see what is in Figure 9-34 now.

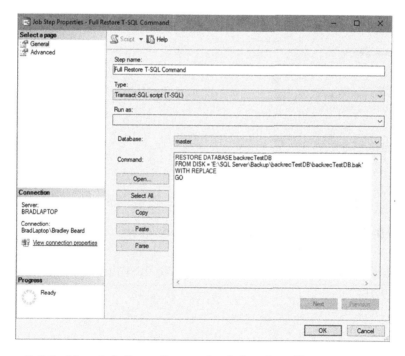

Figure 9-34. *New Job Step, General tab (updated)*

Once this is all filled out, click the OK button to create the preliminary job. Immediately double-click the job again and you will see that the Run as: drop-down menu is now enabled. However, there is no selectable value. We cannot choose to run this job as SQL Server Agent, in other words.

Click the Advanced tab and you will see the screen shown in Figure 9-35.

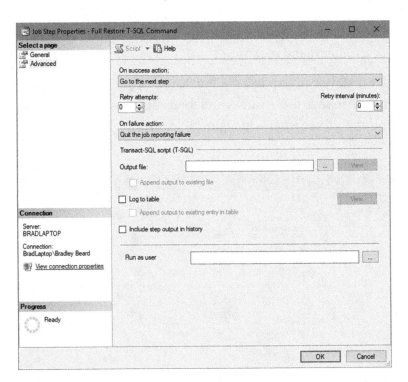

Figure 9-35. *Job Step Properties, Advanced tab*

Again, we need to update these options to the values shown in Listing 9-16.

Listing 9-16. Advanced Tab Options

- On success action

  - Keep this as the default value.

- Retry attempts

  - Keep this as the default value.

- Retry interval (minutes)

  - Keep this as the default value.

- On failure action

  - Keep this as the default value.

- Output file

  - Keep this blank, unless you want to create an output file. I don't create them because I am creating the entries in the table and the step output in history, but you are free to do as you wish.

- Log to table

  - Select this option.

- Include step output in history

  - Select this option.

- Run as user

  - Leave this blank. When we do this, the job is forced to run as SQL Server Agent service account.

When you are done, your interface should appear as shown in Figure 9-36.

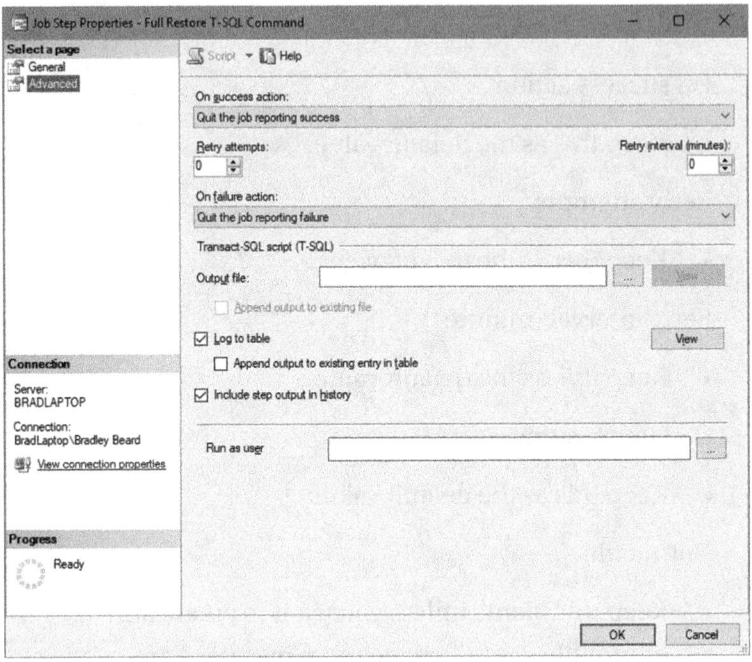

Figure 9-36. *Job Step Properties, Advanced tab (updated)*

These values are all correct, so go ahead and click the OK button to save these configuration settings. We are then returned back to the New Job screen, except with an updated value in the Job step list field. Notice that the Start step value is also updated with the name of the step we just created. Figure 9-37 shows this updated interface.

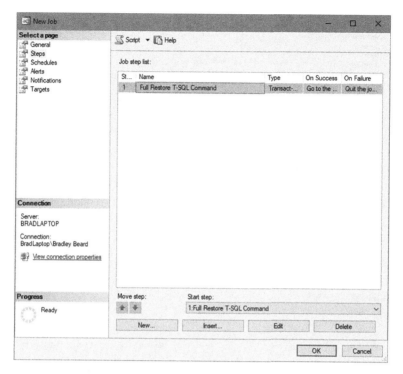

Figure 9-37. *New Job, updated*

We aren't going to schedule this job, and we don't need to set an alert for it either. However, we do want to ensure that the Notifications tab has Write to Windows Application event log checked, and we want to e-mail our Operator that the job was completed—not that it failed and not that is succeeded, but that it completed. This way, we will get the status update either way. Figure 9-38 shows the updated interface for the Notifications tab.

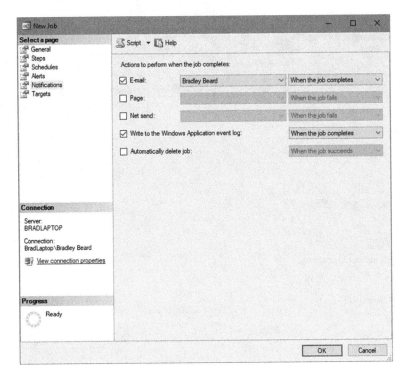

Figure 9-38. *New Job, Notifications tab (updated)*

That is all we need to do to configure this job. Click the OK button to save it and return to the main SSMS screen with the updated job shown in the Jobs submenu of SQL Server Agent. Figure 9-39 shows this updated interface.

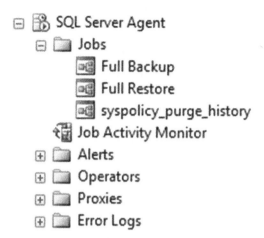

Figure 9-39. *SQL Server Agent, updated*

So in this section, we created an entire restore job from scratch; again, the reason we had to do it like this is because SQL Server does not offer us a restore database tool from the toolbox, so we had to wrap up a RESTORE DATABASE command inside a SQL Server Agent job. Like I said before, if you can get to the end result using an alternate method, excellent!

Copy and Rename Current Backup File

Next, we just need to make a copy of our full backup run previously in this chapter. My default backup location for this database is E:\SQL Server\ Backup\backrecTestDB, but yours may be different. In any event, select the backup location and copy and rename the file as shown earlier. In my case, I am going to rename my file to E:\SQL Server\Backup\backrecTestDB\ backrecTestDB.bak. Once that is done, we can move to the next section.

Restore Data

For this section, all we want to do is right-click the Full Restore Job and select Start Job at Step... to run the job. Note that we need to delete any database snapshots in order to restore the database, so delete any you may have from the SSMS interface before trying to proceed.

Once we run the job, it takes a little while to complete, and then we should see what is shown in Figure 9-40.

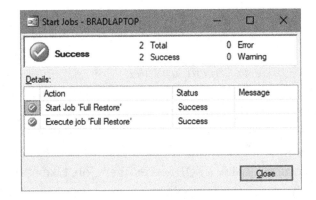

Figure 9-40. *Successfully restored the database*

Next, you can run the Backup and Restore Events report to view that the database was actually restored. You could also check the Windows Application event log for entries, which is shown in Figure 9-41.

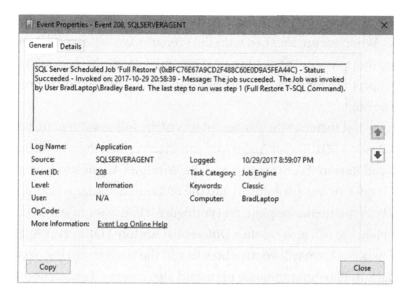

Figure 9-41. *Windows Application event log entry*

So there you have it. A complete full restore job that we can now use to restore our database whenever we need. Just follow the directions in this section and you will be in good shape.

Summary

In this chapter, we pieced together our full backup maintenance plan from what we gathered as requirements throughout the course of this book.

We learned about the many various configuration options in the SSMS maintenance plan area.

We also learned about the configuration options in the SQL Server Agent job area.

We learned how to set up an Operator to receive e-mails in the event of a job failure.

This is the first part of the three parts needed to create an entire backup scenario. When we are finished with the scenario, we will test it extensively to ensure that every event notifies the Operators correctly, so don't worry that we didn't test for the e-mail receipt yet. We will get to this before the book is through.

We also put together the various pieces of the full Restore plan, tested the Full Restore SQL Server Agent job, and then verified the results from the Backup and Restore Events report and the Windows Application event log.

In Chapter 10, we are going to add the differential backups to the Backup Plan maintenance plan, and configure it like we configured the full backup plan. We will also create a Differential Restore SQL Server Agent job.

In Chapter 11, we will go over how to add the transaction log backups to the Backup Plan maintenance plan, and also create a Transaction Log Restore SQL Server Agent job.

The book will conclude with an entire test plan, a guide on how to test the plan for success, and troubleshooting hints and tips that we can use to mitigate harmful situations or errors in our package execution.

CHAPTER 10

Differential Backup and Restore Solutions

Now that we have functional full backup and full restore SQL Server Agent jobs detailed in Chapter 9, we need to piece together the differential backup and differential restore parts. We are going to draw from Chapter 2 and Chapter 6 for this chapter, but we will be looking at adding slightly different functionality and customization to our existing Backup Plan maintenance plan.

What we want to do is rework the backup plan to include the differential portion of the backup, and then create a new Differential Restore SQL Server Agent job to be run manually or in conjunction with the Full Restore SQL Server Agent job. At the end of this chapter, we will have created an addition to our existing plan, tested what we have created so far for that plan, and verified the expected results of the intended operation.

Recently, I was tasked with creating an identical development environment in my work area. You can probably see where I am going with this; because of the serendipitous nature of things, I was able to apply what we are doing now in a real-world scenario, and it worked. I could restore a full database backup to a completely fresh instance of SQL Server with zero trouble, and not only that, I was also able to restore the differential and transaction log backups to the new server as well, so I essentially had zero data loss when transferring to the development server. I find it very reassuring to know that I can quickly and correctly back up and restore the data I am responsible for protecting.

© Bradley Beard 2018
B. Beard, *Beginning Backup and Restore for SQL Server*,
https://doi.org/10.1007/978-1-4842-3456-3_10

Oftentimes, I find myself coming up with "nightmare scenarios" which would force me to think and act quickly and correctly. Now, clearly, there are limitations to these scenarios; they must be squarely rooted in situations where I can influence or control the outcome, for example. A scenario with a down server, for example, is squarely out of my responsibility since I rely on someone else to remedy the situation. But, for instance, if I ran a query on accident and wiped out or dropped a table, or my database suffered a SQL injection attack (it can't, but remember this is a nightmare scenario), or some other SQL Server–related issue arose, I need to know that I have the technical acumen to answer the questions that I need to answer. In my mind, there are different steps that we can take to mitigate these nightmare scenarios, and we will hopefully end up addressing these in this chapter.

For now, let's concentrate on adding the differential backup to the Backup Plan maintenance plan we started in Chapter 9.

Adding a Differential Backup in SSMS

The first things that we need to do is open our maintenance plan for editing. In Object Explorer, expand the Management menu and double-click Backup Plan. This opens the maintenance plan, so we can configure any options in the plan. Figure 10-1 shows the initial screen you should see when opening the maintenance plan.

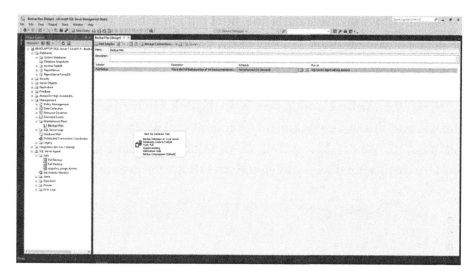

Figure 10-1. *Backup plan main stage*

We need to open up our Toolbox, so either click the Toolbox floating menu on the left or press Ctrl+Alt+X to open your Toolbox. Next, we want to drag another Back Up Database Task to the main stage, to the right of the existing Back Up Database Task. Figure 10-2 shows the approximate location of the new task.

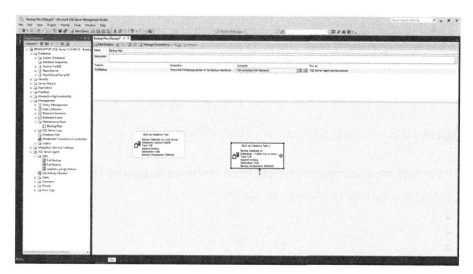

Figure 10-2. *New task*

Just anywhere on the stage is fine, but I put mine there so I can draw the distinction in my mind as a hierarchy; the item to the left is the highest level, and the item to the right is the next level down from the item to the left.

Notice that we have another red X on the task that we need to contend with. We had this same situation in Chapter 9, and we are going to deal with it just like we did then as well. We can start by double-clicking the new task we just put down, and Figure 10-3 shows the default interface.

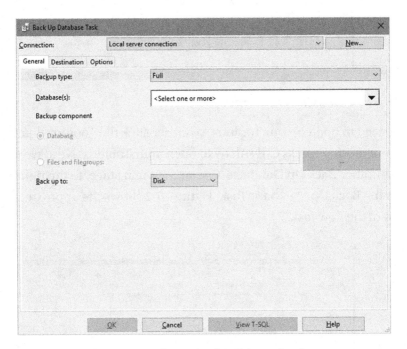

Figure 10-3. *Back Up Database Task, General tab*

For this area, we need to follow what is shown in Listing 10-1 in order to set up the various options in this area.

Listing 10-1. To-Do List

- Backup type

  - We must choose from full, differential, or transaction log. In this case, we are going to choose differential.

- Databases

  - We must choose at least one database. Note that simple recovery model databases are removed if transaction log is chosen from the backup type option. In this case, we are going to choose the database we have been working in, backrecTestDB.

- Backup component

  - We can choose from database or files and filegroups. In this case, we are going to choose database.

- Back up to

  - We must choose from disk, tape, or URL. In this case, keep it set to disk.

Notice that these settings are nearly identical to those from Chapter 9. The only change we made was to select differential instead of full in the Backup type field. Your screen should now look like Figure 10-4.

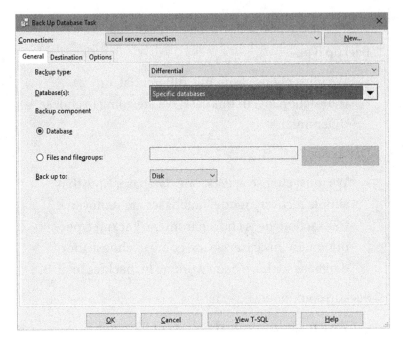

Figure 10-4. Back Up Database Task, General tab, updated

Next, we want to click the Destination tab at the top of the window. Ensure that the Create a sub-directory for each database check box is checked, and that is all we need to do to this tab. Figure 10-5 shows the completed interface.

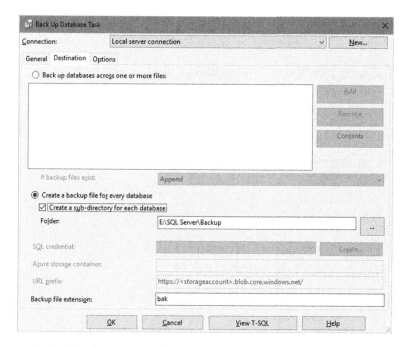

Figure 10-5. *Back Up Database Task, Destination tab*

Click the Options tab next. Again, much like customizing the Full Backup portion of the maintenance plan, we are going to select the Verify backup integrity and Perform checksum check boxes on this tab. Figure 10-6 shows the completed interface.

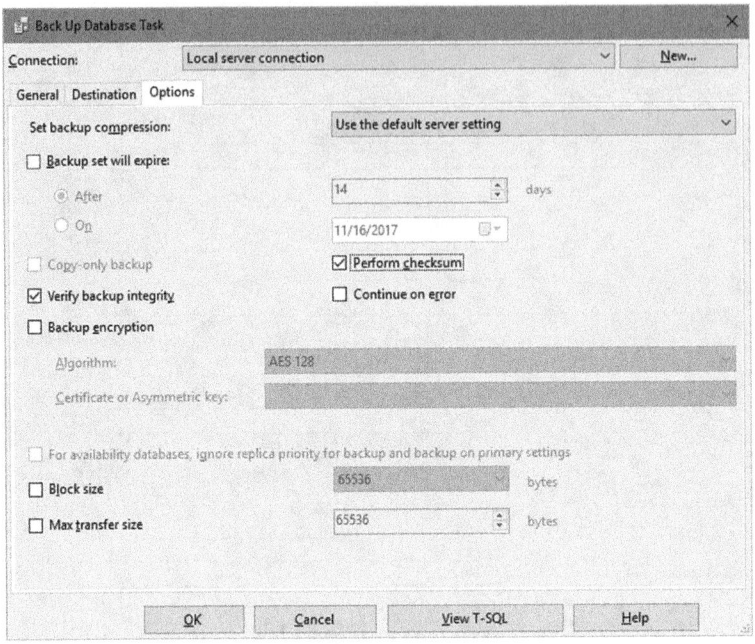

Figure 10-6. *Back Up Database Task, Options tab*

Nicely done! Believe it or not, this is already complete. Next, we need to schedule this part of the plan (sly reference to Dan Fogelberg there). Go ahead and click the OK button to add this part of the task, and notice that the red X has gone away. However, see how we have both tasks in the same stage? Let's do that more efficiently. At the top of the stage, there is a button labeled Add Subplan. Go ahead and click that button, and you will see what is shown in Figure 10-7.

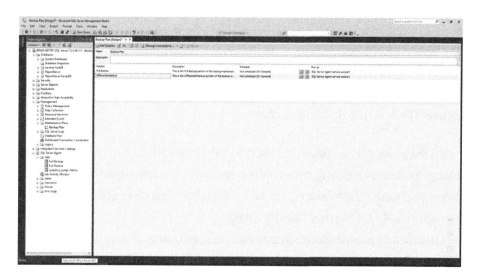

Figure 10-7. *Subplan Properties*

Change the Name field to Differential Backup and add a description of "This is the Differential Backup portion of the backup maintenance plan." Click OK when you are done with this, and you will see an updated interface as shown in Figure 10-8.

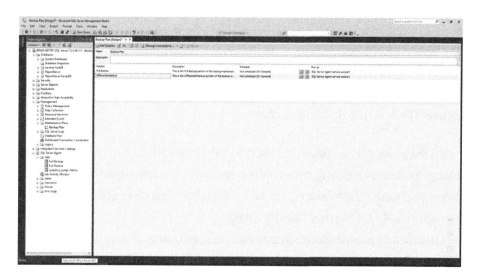

Figure 10-8. *Updated main stage*

Nothing is on the stage right now, because nothing has been added to the subplan. Click back on the Full Backup subplan from the upper portion of the screen, click the subplan we just created, press Ctrl+X to cut the task, select the Differential Backup subplan again, click inside the stage, and press Ctrl+V to paste the task. This will transfer the entirety of the task from the Full Backup subplan to the Differential Backup subplan. Figure 10-9 shows what your updated interface should look like at this point.

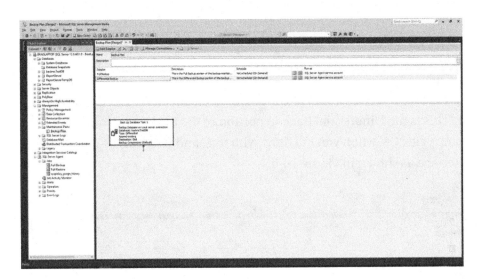

Figure 10-9. *Updated main stage*

So there we go; we have our tasks in the correct subplans, where they belong. You can also long press on the text Back Up Database Task 1 in this screen to change the name of the task. I did this, and changed the task title to simply read Differential Backup Task.

One thing I found interesting about this section was that the full backup schedule did not seem to be retained. Referring back to our original plan for the backups, we need to set the full backup schedule to run at 12:00 AM, and our differential backups need to run every six hours.

Scheduling the Differential Backup

With the Differential Backup subplan selected in the top area, we want to click either the calendar in the menu bar or the calendar in the Differential Backup row. Whichever one you pick will open the same interface. Figure 10-10 shows the initial New Job Schedule window.

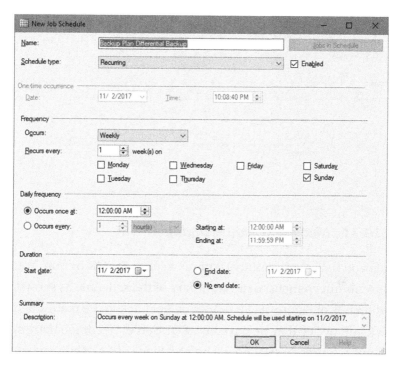

Figure 10-10. *New Job Schedule*

I explained these options in detail in Chapter 9, so I don't need to repeat them here. Instead, you should update your settings to those shown in Figure 10-11, which is to run the differential backup every six hours of every day.

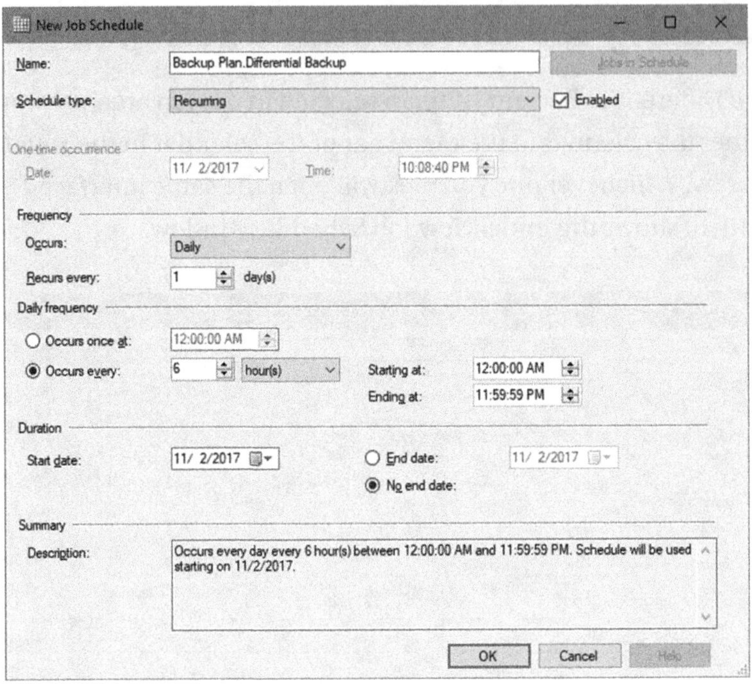

Figure 10-11. *New Job Schedule, updated*

When you have these settings complete, click the OK button. Your Schedule column changes to the summary of the schedule as shown in the Description box of Figure 10-11. Once you get back to the main stage, save your work and notice that we have new SQL Server Agent job names, even for the items we already saved once before. Figure 10-12 shows what this section looks like now.

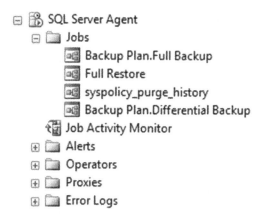

Figure 10-12. *SQL Server Agent, updated*

Let's keep the given names for now, but we will change them later.

Notice that the Full Restore job was not changed? This is because we created this job exclusively within SQL Server Agent, and not from the maintenance plan stage or interface, so this interface did not factor into the naming process of the SQL Server Agent job.

Updating the SQL Server Agent Job

Now that we can see our new Differential Backup job, we need to configure it. We will follow most of the directions from the Full Backup portion of the job, with some slight changes, as noted in the following sections.

General Tab

Nothing needs to be changed on this tab. We have the default settings that carried over from the maintenance plan portion of the job creation, so we can just use those for now. Figure 10-13 shows the General tab with the default values.

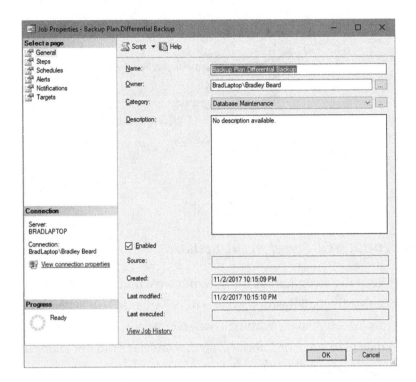

Figure 10-13. *Job Properties, General tab*

Click the Steps menu option on the left to continue.

Steps Tab

The default settings for the Steps tab also are good (Figure 10-14). We can leave these alone, since they are how we need them to be set. Notice that we aren't going to get into the specifics of the step at this point. If you need more explanation about the various options that this step can perform, then consult Chapter 9, where I detailed every single option inside this area.

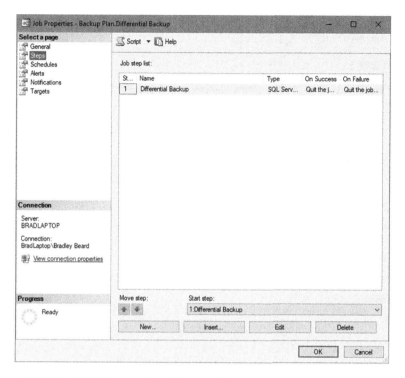

Figure 10-14. *Job Properties, Steps tab*

Click the Schedules tab to continue.

Schedules Tab

This tab lets us set up the schedule for the job. Fortunately, this area is already set up as well! Figure 10-15 shows the default settings for this screen.

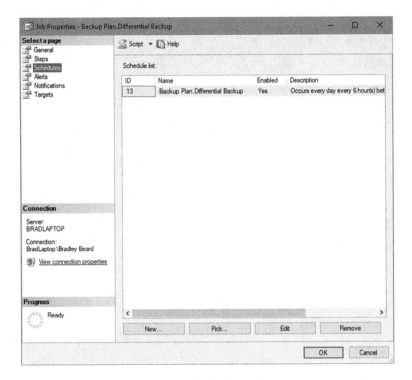

Figure 10-15. *Job Properties, Schedules tab*

Click the Alerts tab to check those settings next.

Alerts Tab

This tab is blank, because we aren't using any alerts for this job. Go ahead and skip over to the Notifications tab next.

Notifications Tab

Much like for the full backup plan, I want to be e-mailed if this plan ever fails. In order to accomplish that, I first need to have an Operator set up, and then I must have the notifications enabled and configured correctly in this area. Figure 10-16 shows the updated values that should be present in your area.

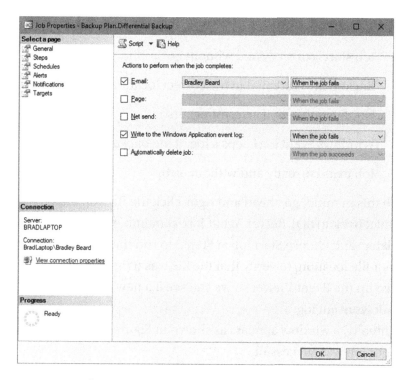

Figure 10-16. *Job Properties, Notifications tab*

That is the conclusion to this section. We have successfully set up the Differential Backup job. Go ahead and click OK to continue with the next section.

Testing the Differential Backup Plan

Chapter 9 had us create the Full Backup plan, and then test it. If you followed along, your plan should have tested successfully as well. Next, we only want to run the Differential Backup portion of the plan, but before we get to that point, we need to determine the exit criteria for the plan. In this instance, Listing 10-2 details what we will be looking for as exit criteria.

Listing 10-2. Exit Criteria

- Job starts correctly and without error

- Backup file is created in the correct location

- Notification sent if an error occurs

- Windows event log keeps a log of the backup operation

- Job exits correctly and without error

With this in mind, go ahead and right-click the Backup Plan. Differential Backup SQL Server Agent Job (remember, we will change the names later) and choose Start Job at Step... to run the job. You can also open your file location, to verify that the file was written as expected, and also open up the Event Viewer so we can see if a new entry was added to the Windows event log.

Eventually, a window appears as shown in Figure 10-17, which shows us that our job was successful.

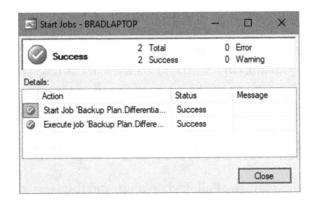

Figure 10-17. *Start Jobs success*

I also got an entry in the Application log of Windows Event Viewer, the details of which can be seen in Figure 10-18.

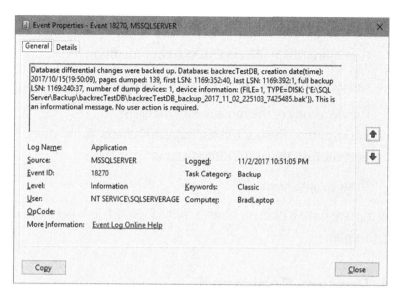

Figure 10-18. *Event Properties*

I also checked the file location, and the new differential backup was created. We can therefore safely assume that the plan is working correctly.

Differential Restore Plan in SSMS

We are going to use SQL Server Agent to create the Differential Restore plan in SSMS, just like we did with the Full Restore plan we covered in Chapter 9. We are going to follow the same basic set of instructions, except where the type of restore is referenced. Listing 10-3 will detail the steps we need to take to ensure our Differential Restore plan executes correctly.

The basic structure for how we plan to implement this is simple, as shown in Listing 9-12.

Listing 10-3. Structure for Restoring Data

- Configure RESTORE DATABASE command(s)

- Create SQL Server Agent Job with T-SQL type

- Create a copy of the most recent differential backup since the last full backup and rename it backrecTestDB_DIFFERENTIAL.bak

- Restore data normally

Now that we have a plan on how to move forward, let's get started on creating this plan.

T-SQL Restore Command

In this instance, we are going to use the T-SQL command shown in Listing 10-4.

Listing 10-4. RESTORE DATABASE Commands

```
RESTORE DATABASE backrecTestDB
FROM DISK = N'E:\SQL Server\Backup\backrecTestDB_FULL.bak'
WITH NORECOVERY, REPLACE;

RESTORE DATABASE backrecTestDB
FROM DISK = N'E:\SQL Server\Backup\backrecTestDB_DIFFERENTIAL.bak'
WITH RECOVERY;
```

Recall that the NORECOVERY attribute lets us specify that we are restoring the last full backup and then the differential backup. We cannot restore a differential backup without first restoring the most recent full backup, so we need to run a full restore first, and then a differential restore. For this reason, we are including the full restore syntax shown in Listing 10-4 along with the differential restore syntax to restore the database correctly. Note that these two commands are separated by a semicolon; this denotes that we are going to use the commands in two separate SQL Server Agent job steps, as shown in the next section.

SQL Server Agent Restore Job

For this section, we will start by creating a new SQL Server Agent job. Expand SQL Server Agent and right-click Jobs, then select New Job... to continue. Once the New Job window opens, update the window with the values shown in Figure 10-19.

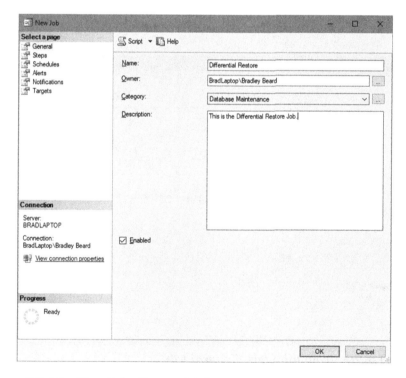

Figure 10-19. New Job, General tab

I want to reiterate that your values will be different from mine, as far as the owner value goes, in this instance. There are probably a lot of instances where your specific user accounts will be different from mine, so the instructions I give should be used conceptually and not in the literal sense. This may be obvious to most, but I wanted to spell that out in case there was any confusion.

Next, we want to select the Steps tab. In this area, we want to click the New... button to open the New Job Step screen and create a new step for the job. The first step that we need to create is the full restore task, and the second task we need is the differential restore. Update the New Job Step screen as shown in Figure 10-20 to create the full restore portion of the plan.

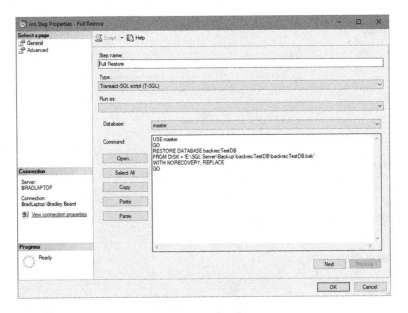

Figure 10-20. *New Job Step, General tab*

Next, click the Advanced tab to show the options in that area. We only want to select the Log to table and Include step output in history check boxes here; the rest of the options can stay as they are by default. Figure 10-21 shows the screen as it should look with updated values.

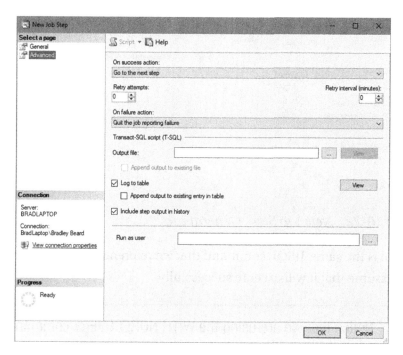

Figure 10-21. *New Job Step, Advanced tab*

When you have those values set, click the OK button to close this window and return you to the New Job window. We can now see the full restore step listed as Step 1.

We need to create the differential restore step now, so click the New... button again to open a fresh instance of the New Job Step window. On this screen, we are going to enter the information as shown in Figure 10-22 to get the differential step set up.

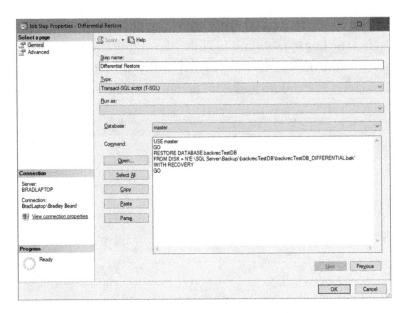

Figure 10-22. *New Job Step, General tab*

That is the same T-SQL command that we referenced earlier, so we can safely assume that it will execute successfully.

Note   Notice that we are using the WITH NORECOVERY command for the full backup step and the WITH RECOVERY command for the differential backup step. This is because the full backup step is going to be immediately followed by the differential backup step, and we are telling the database that we want to keep the database in the Restoring... state until we restore the differential backup step, and then put the database back online with the WITH RECOVERY command in the differential backup step.

Click the Advanced tab now, and update it just as we did in Figure 10-21 earlier. When you have updated the Advanced tab with these options, go ahead and click the OK button to return to the New Job screen shown in Figure 10-23.

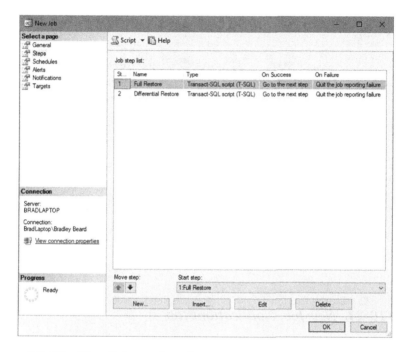

Figure 10-23. *New Job, updated*

We can now see that the full restore job is step 1, and the differential restore is step 2. We can also see that step 1 will move to step 2 on success, which is what we wanted to do as well. That way, the job continues instead of relying on human interaction. After all, the point of these exercises is to increase automation within SQL Server, not to make our jobs more cumbersome.

We don't need to access the Schedules or Alerts tabs, so skip over to the Notifications tab next. We want to select the E-mail and Write to the Windows Application event log check boxes, and then choose the Operator you should have set up in the drop-down menu next to the E-mail check box. The completed values are shown in Figure 10-24.

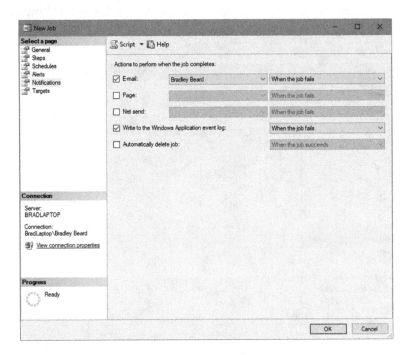

Figure 10-24. *New Job, Notifications tab*

When your screen matches what is shown in Figure 10-24, just click the OK button to return to the main SSMS window. The SQL Server Agent Job has been successfully created, and the Jobs submenu under SQL Server Agent in Object Explorer has now been updated as shown in Figure 10-25.

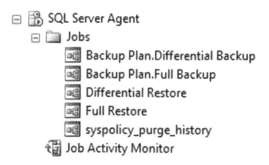

Figure 10-25. *Jobs submenu*

We are now ready to move on to the next section.

Copy and Rename Current Backup

My backup location, E:\SQL Server\Backup, has stayed the same for quite a few years, and will probably stay the same until I stop using SQL Server. I suppose the reason for this is because it is never really a good idea to store backups on the C: drive, and the D drive was usually a CD-ROM or DVD drive, so the physical storage I had available was the E: drive. However this works out for you, just be sure that you are not storing your backups on the boot drive and you'll be fine.

Navigate to your backup location and find the latest differential backup taken. We need to make a copy of this file and rename it to backrecTestDB_DIFFERENTIAL.bak. Once you have copied and renamed that backup, we are ready to execute the backup and see if it works.

Let's make a quick change to the database so that we have something to restore. Remember when we dropped the users1 table? Let's do that again. That should give us a decent amount of data to restore. Note that I would normally recommend that we use transaction log restores to get this data back, but we aren't quite there yet, and this method will work for what we need to have demonstrated.

Restore Data

Right-click the Differential Restore SQL Server Agent job and select Start Job at Step... to execute the job. We are presented with a window shown in Figure 10-26.

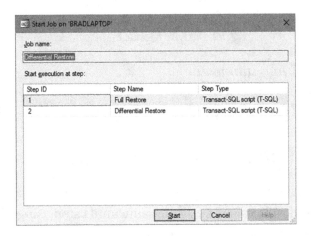

Figure 10-26. *Start Job at Step... screen*

Select the first step, Full Restore, and click the Start button. Eventually, we are shown the success message shown in Figure 10-27.

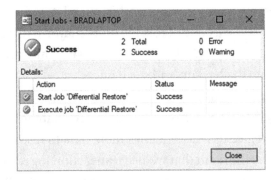

Figure 10-27. *Start Jobs success*

At this point, our database has had the full backup and differential backup applied. Next, we need to verify that the plan restored data correctly, so run the Backup and Restore Events report that we ran earlier to verify. To run this report, right-click your database, go to Reports, and then click the Backup and Restore Events item. Once there, you should see the top two items very similar to what is shown in Figure 10-28.

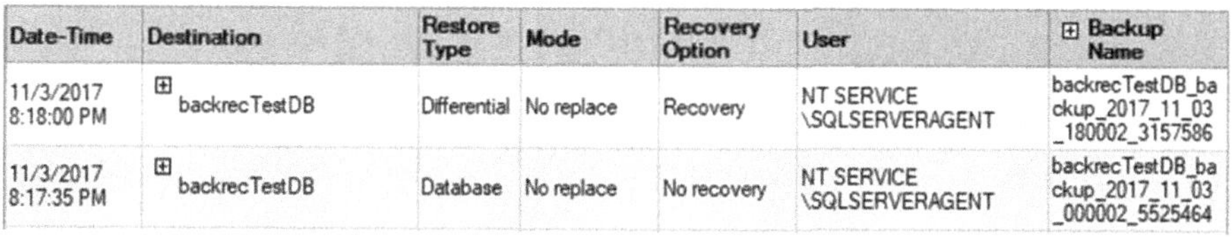

Date-Time	Destination	Restore Type	Mode	Recovery Option	User	⊞ Backup Name
11/3/2017 8:18:00 PM	⊞ backrecTestDB	Differential	No replace	Recovery	NT SERVICE \SQLSERVERAGENT	backrecTestDB_ba ckup_2017_11_03 _180002_3157586
11/3/2017 8:17:35 PM	⊞ backrecTestDB	Database	No replace	No recovery	NT SERVICE \SQLSERVERAGENT	backrecTestDB_ba ckup_2017_11_03 _000002_5525464

Figure 10-28. *Successful restore operations*

This tells us that the first operation was the bottom one, and the last operation was the top one. The first operation was the full restore (we can tell because it says the Mode was "No recovery") and the second operation was the differential restore.

Another way that I can tell that the database was restored correctly is that the users1 table has been restored to the Tables list. The Application event log also shows the entry, so I am assuming that the differential restore operation was a success.

Summary

In this chapter, we went over the basics of how to back up and restore differential data from SQL Server Management Studio. We learned the T-SQL portion of the RESTORE DATABASE command and what the WITH NORECOVERY and WITH RECOVERY commands do. We went over the steps to restore differential data using the most current differential backup, and we also learned how to verify that the differential restore was completed successfully.

In the next chapter, we are going to go over transaction log backup and restore solutions, which will enhance the Backup Plan maintenance plan that we have been building throughout this book. At the conclusion of that chapter, you will have a very good understanding of how to back up data from SQL Server, and more importantly, how to restore that data to SQL Server and then verify that the data was restored correctly and as expected.

CHAPTER 11

Transaction Log Backup and Restore Solutions

In this section of the book, we have looked at complete backup and restore solutions for full and differential types. We saw how the differential restore type used the full restore type as the base for the restore, and then restored up to the point that the differential backup was taken. In this chapter, we will go over how to complete the third part of the individual backup and restore plans, the transaction log.

We looked at transaction logs and how they work in Chapters 3 and 7, respectively. The obvious purpose of transaction logs is to keep a log of transactions, but they are also used to define a quantifiable section of time in which transactions are located. It is more than just a cluttered stash of random data, in other words; it is a precise record of events as seen by the database, in chronological order. This is how we can rewind the database back to a specific transaction, or apply all changes between certain hours to a differential or full restore operation. This precision is not possible in any way unless you are extremely lucky and happen to be able to restore exactly to the point that a full or differential backup is restored. Otherwise, you will be limited to only the data stored as a part of the full or differential restore operation, which does not give us the precision that is needed to

© Bradley Beard 2018
B. Beard, *Beginning Backup and Restore for SQL Server*,
https://doi.org/10.1007/978-1-4842-3456-3_11

restore to a specific point in time. The chances of this happening are very, very low though, and for that reason, we rely on transaction logs to help us restore important data with great accuracy to the point that is required for our application or our SLA.

In our previous chapters in this section, we basically restored a huge chunk of data in the form of either a full restore or a differential restore. I had an instructor one time tell the class I was in that restore methodologies are like a birthday cake; lots of layers, but really just two main parts: the very large majority of the data (the baked cake portion), and the minutiae of the data (the frosting). In other words, you can certainly have a great cake without frosting, but frosting is so good and really complements the cake. It may not be the best analogy, but it makes sense in my mind because I can visualize a cake without frosting as still a cake, but not really complete; whereas, a cake with frosting... now that's a cake!

To begin this chapter, we again need to have a clear understanding of what we want to accomplish. Typically, we can have a backup routine ready to go in a very short amount of time. The real difficulty comes when we have to deal with restoring the transaction log. For this reason, we need to go about the backup slightly differently than we have in the past with the full and differential backups. Listing 11-1 shows the steps we are going to take to create the transaction log backups. This is an easy process, especially since we have already done most of the steps in Chapter 3, so now we need to enhance what we learned in that chapter into a workable solution that we can use with our full backup plan. Back in Chapter 3, we determined that we want to have transaction log backups run every hour, so that the maximum amount of data that we can lose is minimal. When we restore the transaction log, remember that we have the option of backing up the tail of the log, which contains the most recent transactions, so we could use the point-in-time restore feature to restore up to the exact point of failure.

Adding a Transaction Log Backup in SSMS

I can imagine that this is starting to look a bit familiar at this point. We are going to add the transaction log portion to our existing Backup Plan maintenance plan. Recall that we already have the full and differential portions of the maintenance plan, so this will be the last part that needs to be added in order to complete our backup plan. I have outlined a few important things in Listing 11-1 to keep in mind for this section.

Listing 11-1. To-Do List

- Transaction log backups are going to be run every hour, on the hour

- We will only have a maximum of five transaction logs that can be restored between differential backups

These items I have labeled as our "to-do list" for this section because we need to ensure that we are meeting these goalposts before we can accept the section as complete.

To add the transaction log portion of the maintenance plan, open up the Backup Plan maintenance plan in Object Explorer so that the plan is displayed in the main stage of SQL Server Management Studio, as shown in Figure 11-1.

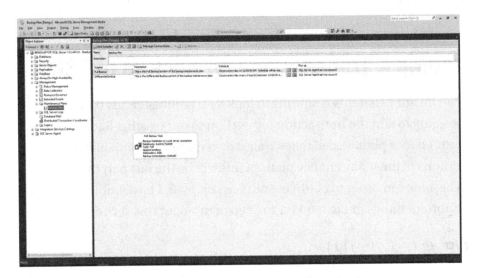

Figure 11-1. *Backup Plan*

Next, we want to click the Add Subplan button shown at the top of the screen. When the Subplan Properties window appears, add the following values in the applicable fields:

- Name: Transaction log backup

- Description: This is the transaction log backup portion of the backup maintenance plan.

We don't want to alter the schedule or the Run as options at this time, since we will get to that shortly. You should now see what is shown in Figure 11-2 in the Subplan Properties window.

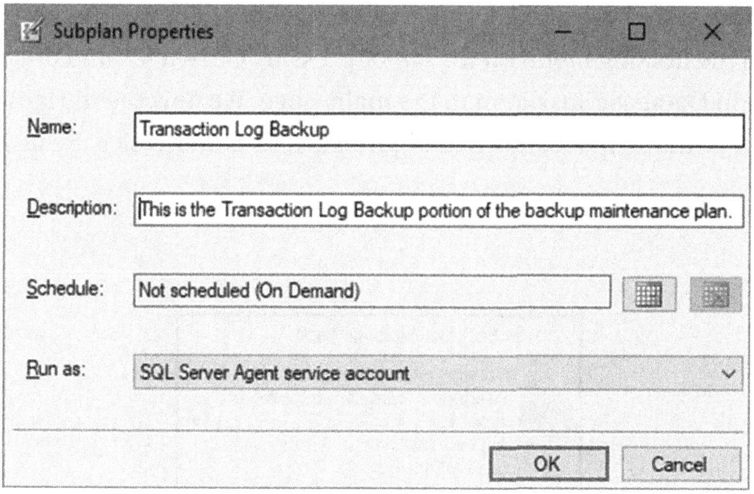

Figure 11-2. *Subplan Properties*

Click OK after this information is entered. Notice that the main stage updates as shown in Figure 11-3 to add the transaction log backup as a new subplan. Also notice that the transaction log backup subplan is selected and there is nothing in the main stage, since this is an entirely new portion of the maintenance plan.

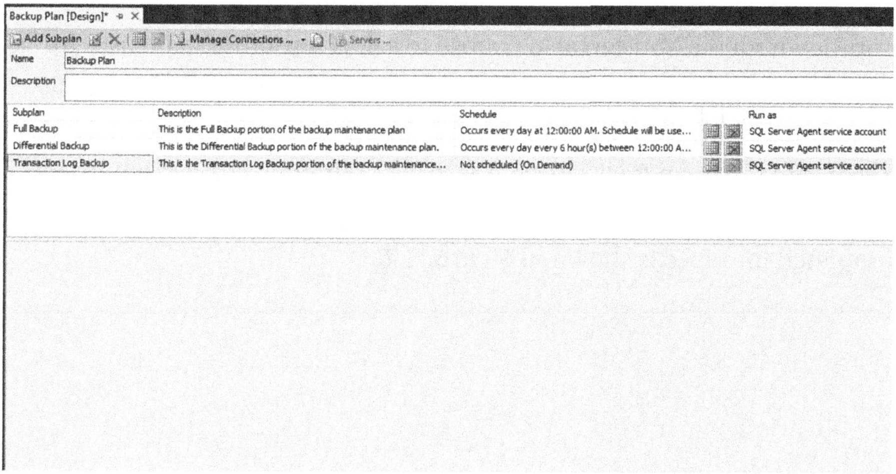

Figure 11-3. *Backup Plan, updated*

Now that we have a blank space to work with, open the Toolbox by clicking the floating menu on the left or pressing Ctrl+Alt+X and dragging a Back Up Database Task item to the main stage. We now see the familiar interface with the red X shown in Figure 11-4, so double-click the task to edit it.

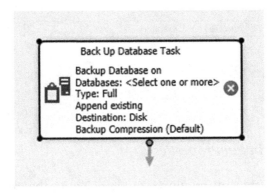

Figure 11-4. *Back Up Database Task*

Once the Back Up Database Task window opens, you will need to choose transaction log in the backup type drop-down menu. Next, you need to select backrecTestDB (or your database) from the Database(s) drop-down menu. You can also choose to select any other databases in this area as well, but we are dealing specifically with our database at this point. Once you have selected the databases you need, click the OK button to return to the main Back Up Database Task window. The last option on this tab, Back up to, should be left as the default option, which is Disk. The completed interface is shown in Figure 11-5.

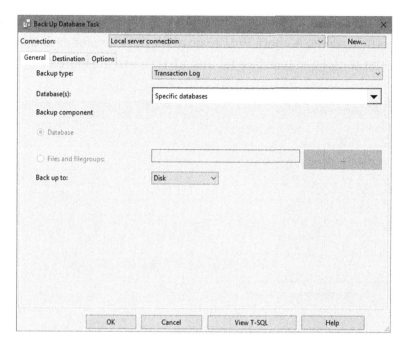

Figure 11-5. *Back Up Database Task, General tab, completed*

Did you notice that once you chose a database, the Backup component selections become disabled? This is because you have selected the transaction log option, so you clearly cannot select a backup component other than the transaction log.

Select the Destination tab in this window to continue. All we want to do in this next screen is check the Create a sub-directory for each database option. The completed interface for this tab is shown in Figure 11-6.

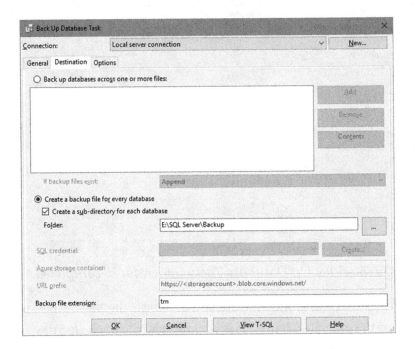

Figure 11-6. *Back Up Database Task, Destination tab, completed*

This simple selection tells SQL Server that we do not want our transaction logs thrown into a single folder; instead, we want them segregated by the name of the database. This is going to make it easier to restore and manage, when needed.

Select the Options tab next, and recall that the options we want to select are as follows:

- Verify integrity

- Perform checksum

These options will ensure that we are verifying our backup and making sure that the backup is going to be checked for errors. Figure 11-7 shows the completed interface for this tab.

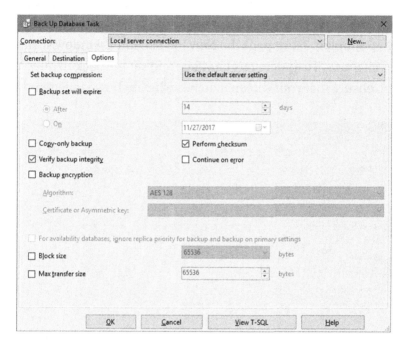

Figure 11-7. *Back Up Database Task, Options tab, completed*

Once you have updated this tab, click the OK button to close this window and return to the main stage. Notice that the red X disappears from our Back Up Database Task item on the main stage. This indicates that this task is free from the basic errors that would have impeded a successful launch earlier when the red X was present.

Next, we need to set up the schedule for this task.

Scheduling the Transaction Log Backup

Just like with the previous subplans we set up in Chapters 9 and 10, we need to click the calendar on the line of the subplan that we want to update. In this case, we are going to choose the calendar on the transaction log backup subplan. This opens the New Job Schedule window seen in previous chapters. To update this interface and set the backup interval to one hour, ensure that your screen matches what is shown in Figure 11-8.

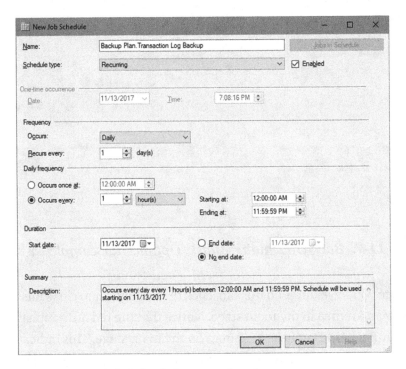

Figure 11-8. New Job Schedule, completed

To complete this interface, I selected the Daily option in the Occurs drop-down menu, then chose the Occurs every radio button and left the default to 1 hour(s). That is all that is required to complete this screen.

Once you have updated this interface, click the OK button to close this window and be taken back to the main stage once again. Figure 11-9 shows what our updated maintenance plan looks like.

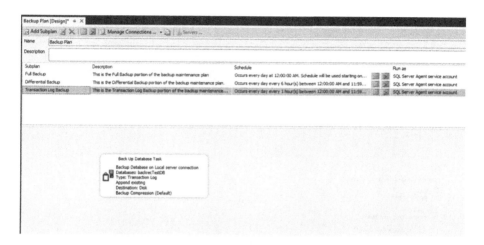

Figure 11-9. *Backup Plan, updated*

Notice the addition of the Schedule information in the transaction log backup subplan entry. That indicates that our schedule information has been entered and retained by the maintenance plan.

Updating the SQL Server Agent Job

Once we finish setting up the main portion of the maintenance plan in SSMS, we need to update a few features in the Jobs section of SQL Server Agent, so expand SQL Server Agent in Object Explorer, then expand Jobs, then double-click Backup Plan.Transaction Log Backup.

General Tab

We start on the General tab, so update it as shown in Figure 11-10.

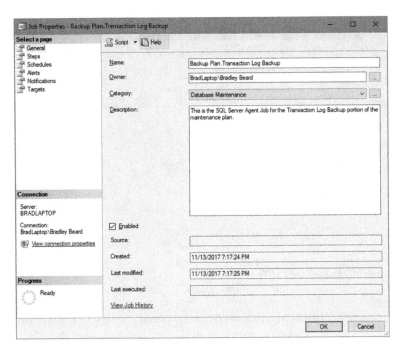

Figure 11-10. *Job Properties, General tab*

All I really did here was update the Description field and verify that the Enabled check box is checked. That's all we need to do to complete this tab. Click the Steps tab to continue.

Steps Tab

This tab already has the transaction log backup job in the job step list area.
We need to update the job though, so double-click the name of the job
and click the Advanced tab. Figure 11-11 shows the updated Advanced
tab; note that the General tab is the default interface, but we don't need to
update anything on this tab.

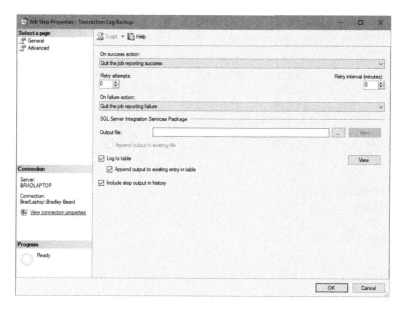

Figure 11-11. *Job Step Properties, Advanced tab*

On this tab, I checked the bottom three check boxes to enable logging
and collection of historical step information. Everything else stays the
same in this screen, so click OK to continue. You will end up back at the
default view of the Steps tab.

We can bypass the Schedules and Alerts tabs since we aren't going to
configure these options. Instead, click the Notifications tab to continue.

Notifications Tab

The default option selected in this tab is to write to the Windows
Application event log. That is a good start, but we want to be notified by
e-mail if the job fails. To enable this, select the E-mail check box, and then
select the Operator (which should have been set up already). Figure 11-12
shows the updated interface for the Notifications tab.

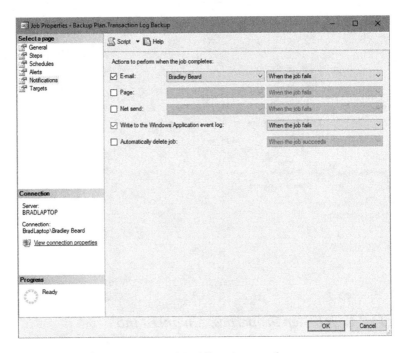

Figure 11-12. *Job Properties, Notifications tab*

Setting this tab up like this will let us be notified by e-mail if the job
fails, and also with an entry to Windows Application event log. This will
complete this section, so go ahead and press the OK button to continue on.
We are returned to the main stage, with our completed backup plan in the
stage. Save your work to the maintenance plan now.

Testing the Transaction Log Backup Plan

To test the transaction log backup plan, we want to right-click the Backup Plan.Transaction Log Backup Job and select Start Job at Step... to fire the job. It should take a very short amount of time to run, and then show a completed status window like the one shown in Figure 11-13.

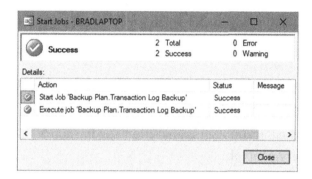

Figure 11-13. *Start Jobs Success*

There really isn't a lot to back up from the transaction log, which is why it takes a very short amount of time to run. Once you see the screen shown in Figure 11-13, you can safely assume that the transaction log backup portion of the Backup Plan maintenance plan has been configured correctly. Verify that a backup was created by checking your backups folder (mine is E:\SQL Server\Backup\backrecTestDB) for the .trn files to be present. If they are in that location, then you are done. If not, then you may need to go back through this first section of this chapter and verify that you created the transaction log backups to be placed in the correct directory.

Transaction Log Restore in SSMS

We are going to use SQL Server Agent to create the transaction log Restore plan in SSMS, just like we did with the full Restore plan we covered in Chapter 9 and the differential Restore plan we covered in Chapter 10. However, we are going to follow a slightly altered set of instructions for the transaction log restores. Listing 11-2 will detail the steps we need to take to ensure our transaction log Restore plan executes correctly.

Listing 11-2. Structure for Restoring Data

- Create a trackable trail of data so that we know what data was restored

- Run the Backup Plan.Transaction Log Backup SQL Server Agent job

- Copy and rename backup files

- Configure RESTORE DATABASE command(s)

- Restore the most recent full backup

- Restore the most recent differential backup

- Restore the transaction logs in order, to the desired point in time

In this scenario, we need to first restore our full backup, then our differential backup, and finally, our transaction log backups in order. This will allow us to restore the data that we need and that is contained within the transaction logs currently backed up. We can use T-SQL to restore to a point in time using our transaction logs by utilizing the STOPAT attribute in our RESTORE DATABASE command. We will go over the syntax for this command very shortly.

Given the backup scenario that I have been pushing throughout this book, it is important to note that we will only ever have to restore a maximum of five transaction logs for each restore sequence, given that we run differential backups every six hours. For this reason, as we noted in Listing 11-1, we need to make sure that when we implement the transaction log backups like we did in the previous section, they are run in the sequence noted earlier (i.e., one transaction log backup is run every hour, on the hour). Utilizing this sequence will allow us to have a maximum of five transaction logs that we can restore without moving to the next chronological full or differential backup to restore from.

Now that we have a plan on how to move forward, let's get started on creating this plan.

Creating Test Data

What we want to do is make some changes to one of our tables so we can see what happens when we restore the database to a point in time. To do this, we need to insert some fake data into our users2 table. Listing 11-3 shows the T-SQL that we will use to accomplish this.

Listing 11-3. Create Test Data

```
INSERT INTO users2
SELECT TOP 1000 * FROM users2
```

Keep a close eye on the time when you run the command in Listing 11-3, because we are going to run that same code a few more times until we have successfully added a substantial amount of data. This will ensure that we are restoring to the correct point in time.

As a point of reference, the row count before running the script in Listing 11-3 was 10000. After running the script one time, it was 11000. Running the script each additional time increased the row count by 1000 rows, so just make sure that you keep an eye on the time and your final row count. When I was done inserting records, I ended up with 29000 records in my users2 table, up from 10000. I only wanted 16000 records though, and I know I had this number of records at 9:22 PM, so I need to restore my transaction logs up to 9:22 PM.

Back Up the Transaction Log

Next, we need to back up the transaction so that the transactions we just carried out are available to us. The time as of this writing is 9:30 PM, so I need to restore the 7:00 PM, 8:00 PM, and 9:00 PM transaction logs, along with the transaction log that we are about to create. Right-click your Backup Plan.Transaction Log Restore SQL Server Agent Job and select Start Job at Step... to execute the job. It runs for a second, and then successfully completes. Click the Close button once it completes, and you are returned to the main SSMS stage.

Copy and Rename Backup Files

The purpose of copying and renaming our backup files is so we don't overwrite our original backup data. There really is no other reason, to be honest. I want to be as careful as possible with my backups, so I will always leave the original file in place and copy and rename when applicable.

Recall that my backup directory is located at E:\SQL Server\Backup\ backrecTestDB, in this situation. When I navigate to that directory, I can see my backup files, including the transaction log I just backed up. I want to copy the logs I noted previously and rename them to chronological names in the format backrecTestDB_1.trn, backrecTestDB_2.trn, and backrecTestDB_3.trn. These three files will represent our three separate transaction logs that we need to restore.

In the end, I have copied and renamed six files, as shown in Listing 11-4.

Listing 11-4. Copy and Rename Files

- Full backup

  - `backrecTestDB_FULL.bak`

- Differential backup

  - `backrecTestDB_DIFF.bak`

- Transaction log backups

  - `backrecTestDB_1.trn`

  - `backrecTestDB_2.trn`

  - `backrecTestDB_3.trn`

  - `backrecTestDB_922PM.trn`

In Windows Explorer, my files appeared as shown in Figure 11-14.

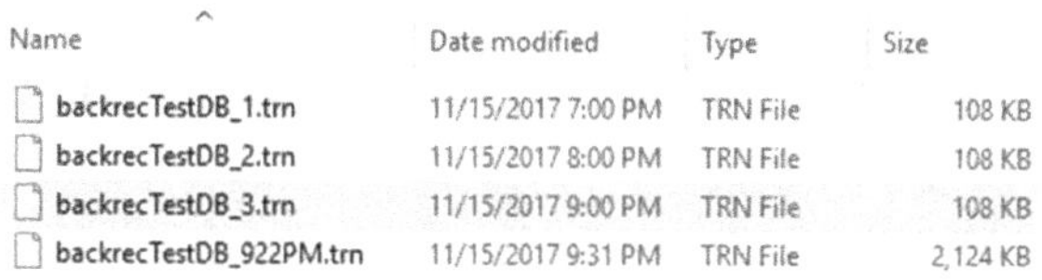

Name	Date modified	Type	Size
backrecTestDB_1.trn	11/15/2017 7:00 PM	TRN File	108 KB
backrecTestDB_2.trn	11/15/2017 8:00 PM	TRN File	108 KB
backrecTestDB_3.trn	11/15/2017 9:00 PM	TRN File	108 KB
backrecTestDB_922PM.trn	11/15/2017 9:31 PM	TRN File	2,124 KB

Figure 11-14. *Windows listing of files*

Note the last transaction log; see how it is much larger than the others? This is the log with all the changes that we just made from Listing 11-3. Next, we will put the commands together to restore our data.

T-SQL Restore Command

Back in Chapter 7, we looked at a T-SQL command in Listing 7-3 that allowed us to restore a full backup, then a differential backup, and then the transaction log backups, in chronological order, until completion. The only real tricky part with restoring data is to keep aware of whether or not you need to use WITH RECOVERY or WITH NORECOVERY.

So how do you know when to use WITH RECOVERY or WITH NORECOVERY? You first have to determine what you need to restore.

Scenario 1: Full Restore

If you're restoring a single full backup, for example, then you should use WITH RECOVERY because this command restores the database and then brings the database out of the restoring state.

Scenario 2: Full and Differential Restore

If you are restoring a full backup and a differential backup, then you want to use WITH NORECOVERY on the full restore, which leaves the database in the restoring state and ready to restore more data, and then use WITH RECOVERY on the differential restore, which takes the database out of the restoring database and back ready for regular use.

Scenario 3: Full, Differential, and Transaction Log Restore

This is probably the most common scenario. In this situation, you want to use WITH NORECOVERY on all of the restores: full, differential, and transaction log. At the end of the T-SQL script, you can either have the line RESTORE DATABASE backrecTestDB WITH RECOVERY to put the database back online and take it out of the restoring state, or you can use WITH RECOVERY in the final transaction log restore statement.

Listing 11-5 shows the basic T-SQL command that we are going to use to restore the database from the full to the differential and finally to the transaction log. Note that the code listed in Listing 11-5 is almost identical to Listing 7-3, and we will be customizing it to better fit our needs shortly.

Listing 11-5. Initial RESTORE Script

```
USE master

-- full database restore
RESTORE DATABASE backrecTestDB
FROM DISK = N'E:\SQL Server\Backup\backrecTestDB\backrecTestDB_
FULL.bak'
WITH NORECOVERY, REPLACE

-- differential database restore
RESTORE DATABASE backrecTestDB
FROM DISK = N'E:\SQL Server\Backup\backrecTestDB\backrecTestDB_
DIFF.bak'
WITH NORECOVERY

-- 7:00PM log restore
RESTORE LOG backrecTestDB
FROM DISK = N'E:\SQL Server\Logs\backrecTestDB\backrecTestDB_1.
trn'
WITH NORECOVERY

-- 8:00PM log restore
RESTORE LOG backrecTestDB
FROM DISK = N'E:\SQL Server\Logs\backrecTestDB\backrecTestDB_2.
trn'
WITH NORECOVERY

-- 9:00PM log restore
RESTORE LOG backrecTestDB
FROM DISK = N'E:\SQL Server\Logs\backrecTestDB\backrecTestDB_3.
trn'
WITH NORECOVERY
```

```
-- final log restore
RESTORE LOG backrecTestDB
FROM DISK = N'E:\SQL Server\Logs\backrecTestDB\
backrecTestDB_922PM.trn'
WITH RECOVERY,
STOPAT = 'Nov 15, 2017 09:22:00 PM'
```

With this script, we renamed some files in our backup directory, and
then restored the database successfully using these renamed files. We
utilized the STOPAT attribute in our RESTORE LOG script to successfully
restore to a point in time within our transaction log.

After running the script shown in Listing 11-5 in SSMS, I was indeed left
with 16000 records, just as I intended. Figure 11-15 shows the row count for
the users2 table before the restoration of the data to 9:22 PM, and after.

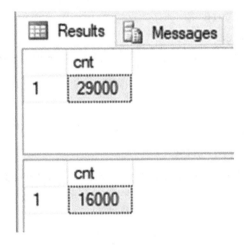

Figure 11-15. *Row count before and after*

Success! We have now been able to restore the database to a point in
time from within SSMS without using the wizard. Note that you can use
the script shown in Listing 11-5 for any number of transaction log restores
(up until the next differential restore) by adding the relevant RESTORE LOG
command and ensuring that the WITH RECOVERY statement is only shown in
the last restore statement.

Summary

This chapter brought this section, and the book, to a close. We were able to successfully restore transaction logs to a point in time using T-SQL within SQL Server Management Studio, we saw how to create test data, and we learned about WITH NORECOVERY and WITH RECOVERY.

I sincerely hope that you have followed along in this book and have learned something new along the way. The lessons in this book are certainly not the entirety of backing up and restoring data within SQL Server, but I believe this book gives you an excellent starting point in becoming more adept at creating an effective backup and restore strategy. There are a lot of concepts in the realm of backing up or restoring data that I didn't touch on in this book; while they are important, I didn't include them because I believe that they would have convoluted the topics I was trying to present. I wanted to make this book the absolute easiest to follow as I could, and I didn't want to talk over anybody's head in the process, so if the content was a bit light, I do apologize. The concepts in this book can be related to either development or production environments though, and I thought it was most important to have a very firm foundation in the rudimentary knowledge of backing up and restoring data before more advanced topics were introduced. I believe that, through the course of this book, your knowledge on the topic has grown to the point where you could continue on comfortably with a more advanced book on this topic and be able to follow along easily.

I encourage you to take these examples and apply them in your work development environment, and concentrate on taking what is here and making it better than it is through automation, for example. There are plenty of great examples that I mentioned in this book, specifically the maintenance script from Ola Hallengren. The second edition of this book will have a comprehensive chapter on this script alone, detailing all the separate pieces to it, since it does merit its own separate section; it really is pretty spectacular.

Congratulations for finishing this book! Now you get to apply what you have learned. I wish you, the reader, all the best in your personal and professional life.

Index

A, B, C

Backup
  database, 203
    destination tab, 65, 206–208
    differential task, 70
    options tab, 66, 209–214
    update, 205, 214
  definition, 4
  recovery model, 5
  and restore, 192–193
  script attributes, 45
  timeline
    backrecTestDB, 153
    update backrecTestDB, 154
  types, 7

D

Database backup
  general tab, 14–15
  manual backing up, 18–20
  transaction log shrunk, 20
Database restore
  instructions, 168–170
  restore script, 170–171
  SQL Server Management
    Studio, 172

status verification, 171–172
  T-SQL, 167–172
Database snapshot
  creation, 188
  frozen point, 191
  logical name location, 189
  querying source, 190
  report, 187
  restore, 191–192
  SQL Server Agent, 188
  subsequent transaction, 187
Data recovery process, 93
Differential backup, 7
  adding to backup solution,
    28–30
  add SSMS, 258
  configuration
    destination tab, 72
    general tab, 71
    job schedule, 74
    options tab, 73
    update job schedule, 75
  definition, 23
  dependency, 24
  job schedule, 267, 268
  preparing for, 30–31
  Restore plan in SSMS, 275

© Bradley Beard 2018
B. Beard, *Beginning Backup and Restore for SQL Server*,
https://doi.org/10.1007/978-1-4842-3456-3

Printed in the United States
By Bookmasters